SECRETS
of the
NECRONOMICON

About the Author

Donald Tyson lives in Halifax, Nova Scotia, and is a professional writer, with numerous nonfiction and fiction books to his credit. His books focus on different aspects of Western occultism, including ceremonial magic, runes, divination, Enochian magic, sexual alchemy, and the Kabbalah. The *Necronomicon Tarot* completes his Lovecraft trilogy that began with *Necronomicon: The Wanderings of Alhazred* (Llewellyn, 2004) and *Alhazred* (Llewellyn, 2005).

About the Artist

Anne Stokes is a freelance illustrator living in Leeds, United Kingdom. She has a passion for realizing the fantastical worlds of her imagination, and her creations have graced innumerable books, T-shirts, packaging, and other merchandise, many within the games industry. To see more of Anne's artwork, visit her website at www.annestokes.com.

Secrets
of the
NECRONOMICON

LLEWELLYN PUBLICATIONS ✦ WOODBURY, MINNESOTA

Secrets of the Necronomicon

Donald Tyson

Illustrated by Anne Stokes

FIRST EDITION
Fifth Printing, 2012

Book design by Rebecca Zins
Cover design by Kevin R. Brown
Cover illustration and interior cards © 2007 Anne Stokes

Llewellyn is a registered trademark of Llewellyn Worldwide Ltd.

ISBN 978-0-7387-1086-0
This book is a component of the *Necronomicon Tarot* kit, which consists of a boxed set of 78 full-color cards and this perfect-bound book.

Llewellyn Worldwide does not participate in, endorse, or have
any authority or responsibility concerning private business
transactions between our authors and the public.

All mail addressed to the author is forwarded. but the publisher
cannot, unless specifically instructed by the author,
give out an address or phone number.

Any Internet references contained in this work are current
at publication time, but the publisher cannot guarantee that
a specific location will continue to be maintained.
Please refer to the publisher's website for links
to authors' websites and other sources.

Llewellyn Publications

A Division of Llewellyn Worldwide Ltd.
2143 Wooddale Drive
Woodbury, MN 55125-2989
www.llewellyn.com

Printed in the United States of America

Contents

THIS TAROT IS based on my own version of the *Necronomicon* (*Necronomicon: The Wanderings of Alhazred* Llewellyn Publications, 2004). Many of the creatures and higher beings depicted on the cards will be familiar to readers of the fiction of H. P. Lovecraft, but some of them appear only in the formerly unrevealed pages of Alhazred's book. Those seeking a deeper understanding of beings not mentioned in Lovecraft's writings should consult my text, where they are described for the first time.

The *Necronomicon Tarot* was designed to be a fully functional tarot deck, suitable for both meditation and divination. I made a conscious effort to avoid turning it into a random picture gallery. Its trumps have the same astrological associations and adhere to the same sequence as the trumps of modern esoteric tarots that follow the Golden Dawn system of correspondences. Suits bear elemental properties that match those of esoteric tarots, as do the court cards, and the suit

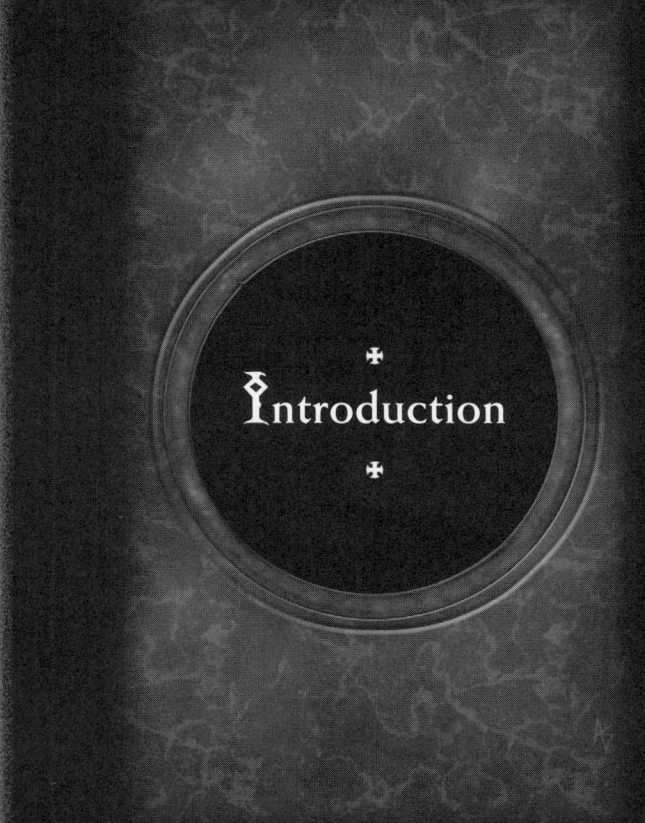

Introduction

symbols resemble the symbols of the regular tarot closely enough to avoid confusion. The prevailing colors of the suits are the colors of the elements linked with the suits in the Golden Dawn system.

This structural similarity with modern esoteric tarots, such as those decks designed by A. E. Waite, S. L. MacGregor Mathers, and Aleister Crowley, allows the *Necronomicon Tarot* deck to be used for serious divination work. The same layouts may be employed, and the same interpretations applied to the cards, as in other major esoteric tarots. It should be kept in mind that the general subject matter of the deck is grim, and this darkness of symbolism will color the results of fortunes told using the tarot. Readings may tend to be bleak and unforgiving if the cards are interpreted in a direct way. A diviner aware of this tendency should compensate for it by seeking an optimistic interpretation when doing readings for others, and should minimize the more gloomy meanings of the cards.

The divinatory meanings for the cards in the text are based on their conventional esoteric interpretations and in some instances are in minor discord with the card images. This is particularly noticeable for the court cards. The conventional interpretations have been provided so that the cards can be read in a divination layout with the usual results, but those who wish to modify their meanings to be more in harmony with the actual images of the *Necronomicon Tarot* will find that they provide a somewhat different set of interpretations that still resonate with the conventional meanings. Let intuition be your guide in this matter.

The general plan of the deck can be described in a few words. The twenty-two picture cards known as the trumps are composed of gods, devils, and monsters that appear in my edition of the *Necronomicon*. They are agents of the cosmic forces that overshadow the world of humanity in the mythology of that work. The court cards are made up of distinct classes of human beings who might be found in the world of my *Necronomicon*. The temptation to introduce more colorful creatures into the court cards was resisted because in tarot divination the court cards represent people, not monsters, and I wished to preserve the practical utility of the deck. The number cards of each suit present a connected narrative in pictures, the theme of which is in harmony with the meaning of the suit.

The number cards of the suits do not possess exactly the same meanings as the number cards of more conventional tarot decks, but if the two are compared, an underlying foundation will be perceived that links them. The suits of the *Necronomicon Tarot* were composed so as to resonate with the suits in modern esoteric tarots that base their meanings on the Golden Dawn system. An understanding of the commonly accepted general meanings of the suit cards will aid in comprehending the particular meanings of the suit cards of this deck.

Each trump bears the number of the card in Roman numerals, except for the trump that is equivalent to the Fool, which carries a zero. The conventional titles for the trumps also appear to avoid confusion, along with titles that are descriptive of the actual scenes. For example, the trump of the Magician bears the conventional title I Magician, along with the descriptive title Nyarlathotep.

The court cards carry only the conventional tarot titles to make their suit and rank immediately obvious. Their unique *Necronomicon Tarot* titles will be found in this booklet. For example, the equivalent to the Queen of Cups bears the conventional title Queen of Cups, but also possesses the unique title Priestess, which you will find in this booklet along with the detailed description of the card. The figures are grouped into themes based on the elemental significance of the suits. Wands, which is the suit of Fire, relates to the human classes of the aristocracy, rulers and overseers. Cups, the suit of Water, is associated with the priestly and scholarly classes. Swords, the suit of Air, is linked with the classes of warfare and lawlessness. Disks, the suit of Earth, is of the classes of magicians and diviners.

The number cards of the suits from Ace to Ten bear only the conventional names for ease of recognition. Their unique *Necronomicon Tarot* titles will be found in this booklet along with their descriptions. The Aces each show an enlarged version of the suit symbol, and multiples of the symbol appear in the following nine number cards. For example, the Nine of Wands, which has the unique descriptive title Stability of Fire, shows nine wand icons in the image on the card. The multiple suit symbols on each number card are not exactly the same as the symbol on the Ace of the suit, but they are of the same general type. All the number cards of the suit of Wands show either pillars, staffs, clubs, or rods, because all of these objects express the essential esoteric quality of the archetypal symbol on the Ace.

The story told by the suit of Wands concerns the mating of the arrogant and aristocratic Atlanteans with the Deep Ones, and the subsequent civil war that resulted in the destruction of Atlantis through the use of crystal energy weapons. The story of the suit of Cups is about an acolyte who experiences the two sides of the Egyptian cult of Bast, the cat goddess, when he becomes a member of that faith. The suit of Swords tells a story of jealousy, violence, and revenge in old Damascus. The suit of Disks presents the preparations and dark ritual of a necromancer who seeks to compel the spirit of a dead woman to reveal the burial place of a strongbox containing a potent mystery.

Users may question the appearance of the Deep Ones in the fiery suit of Wands, rather than in the watery suit of Cups. Although the Deep Ones dwell in the oceans, their nature is generally not in harmony with the suit of Cups, which is associated with tender feelings or affection and love, as well as with religion. The Deep Ones are not particularly loving, but seek to dominate and control. They are linked in my *Necronomicon* with the Atlanteans, who are an arrogant race of slave-owning aristocrats, well adapted to represent the suit of Wands. I considered whether to use the Deep Ones and the Atlanteans in the suit of Cups, but finally decided that these joined races were too overbearing and aggressive to embody the gentle emotions of the water suit, despite of their marine habitat.

Those who seek a fuller understanding of the Deep Ones, and all the other races and creatures depicted on the cards, will find it in my book *Necronomicon: The Wanderings of Alhazred*, and also in my associated novel *Alhazred*, which is based on the events and places described in my *Necronomicon*, but is presented in the words and from the personal viewpoint of the author Abdul Alhazred himself. The images in this tarot deck derive directly from *Necronomicon: The Wanderings of Alhazred*, so serious users are advised to read the book. It is not absolutely necessary to read my novel *Alhazred* to appreciate and use the *Necronomicon Tarot*, but the novel will greatly enhance enjoyment of the deck, because the strange creatures illustrated on its cards are described in great detail in the novel.

This tarot is the third piece in a trilogy of work based on Lovecraft's mythos of the Old Ones. The first part is my interpretation of the *Necronomicon*, the second part my novel *Alhazred*, and the *Necronomicon Tarot* completes the trilogy by providing graphic images of the beings and places in the other books. The three works are meant to be fully appreciated as a group, although each is designed to stand on its own merits.

A close comparison between the card images and the descriptions in this book will reveal minor details in the descriptions that are not found on the cards themselves. These discrepancies result from the process by which the cards were created. The artist,

Anne Stokes, worked from my written descriptions, but for practical reasons she was not always able to incorporate every detail into the card images. Where these descriptive details do not come into actual conflict with the images, I have allowed them to remain on the consideration that they add additional symbolism to the cards that aids in a fuller understanding of their meanings.

THE NECRONOMICON IS best known from references to it that appear scattered throughout the short fiction of the writer Howard Phillips Lovecraft (1890–1937), a native of Providence, Rhode Island, whose stories of eldritch evil dignified the pages of *Weird Tales* and other less prominent pulp magazines in the early decades of the twentieth century. According to reputation, the mere possession of any edition of the *Necronomicon* is dangerous, and those who actually open and read the text may as well abandon hope, so certain is their destruction.

Lovecraft described the book in one of his early tales as "the unmentionable *Necronomicon* of the mad Arab Abdul Alhazred, in Olaus Wormius' forbidden Latin translation; a book which I had never seen, but of which I had heard monstrous things whispered" (*The Festival*, 1925). Alhazred, the reputed author of the work according to Lovecraft, was a mad poet born in the land of Yemen who dwelt

CHAPTER 1

✠

Necronomicon

✠

during his maturity at Damascus in Syria until his public murder by an invisible fiend in that city in 738 CE.

Precisely what drove Alhazred mad is never made clear by Lovecraft, but we may assume it had something to do with the Old Ones, a race of godlike beings from beyond the stars who ruled the Earth in its distant prehistory, and who wait with reptilian patience for the stars to once more come right in their courses, so that they can resume their despotism and enslave humanity. Perhaps because of his insanity, or perhaps due to some circumstance of his birth, Alhazred was gifted with an awareness of the Old Ones and of other equally strange and dangerous creatures who dwell at the edges of reality, seeking entrance to our world. In his old age, the humor moved in him to set his knowledge down in a book. The result was the *Necronomicon*.

The Latin translation of Olaus Wormius is only one edition of the work. Lovecraft made a detailed history of the dread tome in a private communication intended for his own circle of literary friends. He wrote that the original text, titled *Al-Azif* (which some have translated as *Buzzing of Flies*) was penned in Arabic by Alhazred around the year 730, less than a decade prior to his horrible and inexplicable death. So it remained until 950, when the text was translated into Greek by Theodorus Philetas and given its present title *Necronomicon*, which signifies *Customs Concerning the Dead*. Exactly a century later, all known copies of the book were gathered together and burned by Michael Cerularius, Patriarch of Constantinople (ruled 1043–1058). Olaus made his Latin translation from a surviving Greek copy in 1228, all known Arabic manuscripts of the work having perished. Only four years later, Pope Gregory IX (ruled 1227–1241) saw fit to suppress both the Latin and Greek editions of the work.

The Elizabethan scholar and magician John Dee (1527–1608), who owned the greatest library in England, caused a new translation to be made of the work into the English language, but it was never published and is said to survive only in fragments. The Latin translation of Olaus Wormius was printed in Germany in the fifteenth century, and again in Spain in the seventeenth century. A copy of the first is said to be kept secure in the British Museum; copies of the second, less-rare printed version are supposed to reside in the occult collection of the Bibliothèque Nationale at Paris and in the libraries of several prominent universities. The printing history of the Greek text is unclear, but copies are rumored to be in the possession of private collectors, although they are exceedingly scarce.

All this detail provided by Lovecraft about the history of the book is remarkable in light of the flat assertion of scholars that the book does not exist, and never has existed in any edition. Those who persist in believing in the reality of the *Necronomicon* are derided as fools by skeptics, and perhaps this attitude is justified from a purely materialistic viewpoint. Lovecraft's publishing history of the book is completely apocryphal. Balancing the scorn of academia is the quiet assertion of practicing magicians such as Kenneth Grant, the head of the occult society known as the Ordo Templi Orientis, that the Old Ones and other beings described by Lovecraft do indeed exist on their own level of reality, and possess a terrible power that can be harnessed through magic.

If the Old Ones can be said in one sense to exist, so can the *Necronomicon*. There is an occult teaching that concerns the existence of a great astral library that takes many forms, depending on the preconceptions and limitations of those who perceive it, and in this library are all the books that have ever been written, on the earthly plane or any other level of reality. At times the edges of this astral library overlap our world, so that those who browse in musty secondhand book stores, or amid the stacks of the ancient libraries of Europe, or even among the private collections of antiquaries, may find themselves staring at the spines of books that no longer survive, or books that never were written by a living human hand. This is said to happen when those who experience this translation to a higher space lapse into a kind of meditative daydream in which the environment around them grows dim and becomes unreal.

The content of the *Necronomicon* varies between descriptions, so that it may be suspected that different astral editions contain entirely different sections of text. It is not uncommon for celebrated books hand-copied over centuries to acquire additional material that is inserted into the works by the copyists, yet is attributed to the original author. It would explain why some editions of the *Necronomicon* are said to be so much larger than others—assuming, for the sake of discussion, that the work has reality on some higher plane.

The contents fall into two broad categories, based on the fragments and references provided by Lovecraft. The first is a description of the nature and history of the Old Ones, and other races, such as the even more ancient Elder Things and the warlike *meegoh*. Alhazred wrote at length about their activities, abilities, and purposes. The second is a discussion of practical magic with particular emphasis on necromancy, which is the communication with the souls of the dead, the occult use of corpses, and the raising of the dead back to corporeal life.

Most modern re-creations of the *Necronomicon* take the form of grimoires of practical magic, and detail various hierarchies of spirits, their realms of authority, and the ways magic may be used to communicate with them and employ them for mundane purposes. My own version of the work is somewhat unusual, in that it is a travel narrative by Alhazred of the strange places and extraordinary beings he encountered during his worldwide wanderings as a young scholar seeking occult knowledge. It contains all of the fragments of text asserted by Lovecraft to come from the *Necronomicon*, and in this sense is more faithful to the spirit of Lovecraft than any other version, but it also holds a great deal of occult information that Lovecraft never imagined.

The lords of the Old Ones, described at length in my *Necronomicon*, are prominently displayed among the trumps of the *Necronomicon Tarot*, along with more humble creatures of nightmare and several pagan deities with which Alhazred interacted in my version of his book. The suit cards of the tarot present the social classes and general milieu of the world through which Alhazred traveled, with the exception of the suit of Wands, which is concerned with the Deep Ones and Atlantis, a land visited by Alhazred in my version of the book only during astral travel. The adventures of the author's life are given in finer and more personal detail in my novel *Alhazred*. Although I have not relied upon the novel as a source for the tarot, the beings depicted on the tarot are examined in the novel, and both the *Necronomicon* and *Alhazred* should be studied for the most complete understanding of the cards.

Chapter 2

Cthulhu Mythos

THE SYSTEM OF mythology that H. P. Lovecraft drew forth from his nightmares over the course of two decades (1917–1937) and described in his tales of horror was given the collective title of the "Cthulhu Mythos" by one of Lovecraft's close friends, the writer August Derleth. The mysterious book known as the *Necronomicon*, also drawn from dreams by Lovecraft, is central to the Cthulhu Mythos, because the most important revelations concerning the mythos are supposed to have been written on its pages during the early part of the eighth century by the mad Arab poet Abdul Alhazred.

The Cthulhu Mythos has several aspects that set it apart from other more conventional mythologies of gods and monsters. Lovecraft described a series of powerful and highly intelligent alien races that traveled across the gulfs of space or through dimensional portals to colonize the Earth in its distant past, long before the evolution of humanity. These races

are essentially uninterested in human beings, except insofar as we may be used as slaves or as sources of nourishment. They are not evil in the conventional sense, but are beyond good and evil as we know them.

In his tales of horror, Lovecraft postulated that these races have not vanished into the oblivion of the past, but are still present, concealed in deep and secret places where they are protected from the harmful rays of the stars, which have become poisonous to them by virtue of their changing pattern in the heavens. Eventually the stars will "come right" for them once again, as they were in the distant past, and these beings will emerge from their protective hibernation to reclaim the Earth and subjugate its inhabitants to their purposes. In the meantime, it is possible for certain cults of human beings to use rituals of magic to communicate with some of these beings. These cults worship these various Old Ones as gods and look forward to their return.

The first race to come to this planet when it was no more than bare rock and sterile oceans is known as the Elder Race. They are responsible for the origins of life on our world. They created mankind for their amusement, along with the majority of the other species in the seas and on the land. One of the Elder Race is depicted on the trump Strength, overseeing the building of a massive stone wall of a great city by their slaves, the shoggoths, which the Elder Race used as beasts of burden before the shoggoths rose in revolt against them.

During the impossibly long stewardship of the Elder Race upon the Earth, other races came at various times to colonize our world, among them the spawn of Cthulhu that occupied certain volcanic islands in the Pacific Ocean, the time-traveling Great Race of Yith that exist only in our distant past and distant future but not our present, the *meegoh* from the planet Yuggoth, which we know as Pluto, who came to mine this world for its metals, and the monstrously huge Old Ones, who are invisible to unaided human vision.

Certain alien individuals stand out from the rest as once and future lords of our world. Represented in the trumps of the tarot are mighty Cthulhu, who dreams in a deathlike trance beneath the Pacific Ocean; Dagon, the fish god, who dwells beneath the waves and rules over the seagoing race of Deep Ones; crafty Nyarlathotep, who is the messenger of the gods of chaos; Yog-Sothoth, the guardian of all portals between the spheres and dimensions; Shub-Niggurath, the endlessly fertile mother of monsters; Azathoth, the blind idiot god, who pipes on his cracked flute the music that unfolds the threads of time and space; mysterious Yig, the wise and watchful father of all serpents; and the toad-god Tsathoggua, who is served by protean beings with shapeless bodies composed of black ichor.

This mythology of alien races may appear childish to the more materially minded, but it is accepted as real by many occultists, who work with the potent forces of the Cthulhu Mythos in their ritual magic, and are willing to testify to its effectiveness. They do not believe that Lovecraft invented the *Necronomicon* and its contents from nothing, but rather maintain that he drew it forth from the astral realm during his dreams. They hold the view that the mythos describes real beings who have an existence on higher planes of reality, above our material world of three dimensions. These beings are able to interact with our reality, and can communicate with those who ritually summon them.

Lovecraft may have been much more than merely the author of horror stories. He may have been a visionary seer able to peer into the distant past and across dimensions during his disturbingly vivid nightmares, which he experienced throughout his life. Most of the important concepts in his fiction were drawn directly from these nightmares; indeed, some stories are nothing more than unembellished descriptions of his recurring dreams. He did not even have to compose them, since they wrote themselves in his sleep. The *Necronomicon* itself is a dream conception—the name of the book was never invented by Lovecraft, but came to him in a dream. The same it true of the lord of the Old Ones known as Nyarlathotep, who figures so prominently in my novel *Alhazred*—Nyarlathotep was not invented by Lovecraft, but was merely copied from a recurring dream that became one of Lovecraft's short stories.

The true *Necronomicon* may never have existed as a physical literary work, but if it is a book that never lived, it is also a book that refuses to die. Of all the occult texts, it is undoubtedly the most famous, a significant achievement for a book that until recent decades could be found only in the imagination. Its name has been covertly added to the card catalogs of the famous libraries of North America and Europe. Antiquarian book dealers regularly received requests for it from buyers, and some in fits of impish humor even included it in their catalogs. It turns up in the bibliographies of occult texts and in other odd and unexpected places, and all these appearances serve to keep the myth of the book alive and growing.

This persistence of the myth of the *Necronomicon* is a sure indication that it has, at its heart, something more than idle fantasy. The Old Ones speak to us on a very deep level of the subconscious mind. They resonate within us and move us in various ways. They are primal articulations of the vast, chaotic sea of potential from which the universe arose, and from their proximity to the source of creation flows raw power that can be shaped and directed by ritual magic. The trumps of the *Necronomicon Tarot* tap into and embody that power.

You should be aware when you use the *Necronomicon Tarot* that you are manipulating potent occult forces that can have real effects in the world. As Alhazred wrote in the *Necronomicon*, "The Old Ones were, the Old Ones are, and the Old Ones shall be." Those who practice the magic of the *Necronomicon* swear that it brings results. It is sometimes said in modern occult circles that the magic of the Enochian Angels is the most potent and dangerous. Others assert that it is the magic of the squares of Abramelin the Mage that can have the most unexpected consequences for the unwary. A case can be made that the most powerful magic of all is that of the *Necronomicon*, because it opens dimensional doors on the places where the Old Ones wait and watch…doors that may not be easy to close.

THE NECRONOMICON TAROT is designed to be in harmony with the set of esoteric correspondences used by the Hermetic Order of the Golden Dawn. The Golden Dawn was an English Rosicrucian society devoted to the study and practice of Western ceremonial magic that flourished at the beginning of the twentieth century. Its teachings subsequently spread around the world, so that today its correspondences for the tarot are the most widely used and recognized of any occult system. They were developed mainly for ritual magic and meditation, but they are helpful in fortunetelling with the tarot, because they give an additional depth of meaning to the cards.

The Golden Dawn system for the tarot trumps is based on the earliest known text of the Hebrew Kabbalah, called the *Book of Formation (Sepher Yetzirah)*. In this brief Kabbalistic text, which is believed to date from the second century, the twenty-two letters of the Hebrew alphabet are assigned certain occult links with various astrological and elemental

CHAPTER 3

✠

Correspondences

✠

forces. In the late eighteenth century, French occultists noticed that there were twenty-two tarot trumps and also twenty-two Hebrew letters. They linked the two together by assigning the letters to the trumps. The Golden Dawn went a step further and transferred the occult associations of the Hebrew letters that appear in the *Book of Formation* to the tarot trumps.

In the Kabbalistic text, the Hebrew alphabet is divided into three groups of letters: three Mother letters, seven Double letters, and twelve Single or Simple letters. The three Mothers are occultly associated with three of the four esoteric elements: Air, Water, and Fire. The seven Doubles are linked with the seven planets recognized by ancient astrology. The twelve Singles are assigned the twelve signs of the zodiac.

The Golden Dawn system uses the bridge of the Hebrew alphabet to join the tarot trumps to these occult forces. The Hebrew alphabet was applied to the trumps in its natural order of letters, but the Golden Dawn changed the positions of two of the trumps to make them better match the occult forces assigned to them. The trumps Strength and Justice were inverted in their places by the Golden Dawn. This is why in older tarot decks, Justice is numbered VIII and Strength is numbered XI, but in esoteric tarot decks following the Golden Dawn teachings, Strength is VIII and Justice is XI.

You do not need to worry about the Hebrew alphabet. The important connection is between the trumps and the occult forces assigned to the Hebrew letters in the Kabbalah. The letters themselves merely form the bridge. However, I will give the English names of the Hebrew letters and their types so that you can easily see how they join the trumps to the occult forces in the system of the Golden Dawn.

0 Fool — Aleph (Mother) — Air
I Magician — Beth (Double) — Mercury
II High Priestess — Gimel (Double) — Moon
III Empress — Daleth (Double) — Venus
IV Emperor — Heh (Single) — Aries
V Hierophant — Vau (Single) — Taurus
VI Lovers — Zayin (Single) — Gemini
VII Chariot — Cheth (Single) — Cancer
VIII Strength — Teth (Single) — Leo
IX Hermit — Yod (Single) — Virgo
X Wheel — Kaph (Double) — Jupiter
XI Justice — Lamed (Single) — Libra
XII Hanged Man — Mem (Mother) — Water
XIII Death — Nun (Single) — Scorpio
XIV Temperance — Samekh (Single) — Sagittarius
XV Devil — Ayin (Single) — Capricorn
XVI Tower — Pe (Double) — Mars
XVII Star — Tzaddi (Single) — Aquarius
XVIII Moon — Qoph (Single) — Pisces
XIX Sun — Resh (Double) — Sun
XX Judgement — Shin (Mother) — Fire
XXI World — Tau (Double) — Saturn

The use of these correspondences is quite simple. The meanings of the occult forces are applied to the trumps and aid in interpreting the meanings of the trumps. For example, when the trump Strength appears in a divination layout, the astrological meaning of the zodiac sign Leo is applied to the tarot card, in addition to the native meaning of the card. It is an indication of the genius of the Golden Dawn system that the meanings of the zodiac signs, the planets, and the elements harmonize so well with the basic meanings of the trumps themselves. They allow a deeper reading of the trumps in tarot divinations.

You should consult a book on astrology to understand the occult meanings of the signs and planets, so that you can accurately assign these meanings to the trumps. In general, it may be observed that the planets are active in their influence on the trumps, whereas the zodiac signs are more in the background, just as the zodiac provides the static backdrop for the dance of the planets in the heavens.

The elements are usually not treated in astrological texts. Only the three active elements are linked to the trumps; the passive and inert element Earth is not used. Earth is fundamentally different in its nature from the three active elements, as the teachings of Plato in his dialogue the *Timaeus* clearly demonstrate. Plato showed by means of geometry that Fire, Air, and Water could be converted one into the other because they are all based on the same basic building block, but that the geometric building block for elemental Earth is different; as a consequence, none of these higher three elements can be changed into Earth, and Earth cannot be made into any of the higher elements.

Elemental Fire is aggressive and willful, relating to the spirit and to flashes of inspiration that strike like lightning. It burns and purifies the soul. It is what gives the power of command. Elemental Air is active and piercing, quick and nimble, relating to the expression of thoughts, the formulation of ideas in the mind and their voicing on the tongue, or through other forms of communication. Elemental Water is reflective and deep, concerned with feelings and emotions, affection, attachment, visions, and dreams. Elemental Earth is solid and inert, slow to move, stubborn, dependable, unimaginative, rooted in place, and linked with the body and physical health.

Fire—Will
Air—Thoughts
Water—Emotions
Earth—Sensations

The three active elements applied to the trumps were understood by ancient philosophers to exist in realms above the surface of the Earth. Nearest the ground was believed to be a zone of esoteric Water, and above it a zone of Air, and above it a zone of Fire. It is these higher, more tenuous and spiritual elements of the heavens that are applied to the trumps. However, all four ancient elements exist on the surface of the Earth, embodied and expressed in a tangible way through physical substances. Here, the lowest, inert element, Earth, is alongside the lower and more material aspects of Fire, Air, and Water. These four lower, or earthly, elements find their expression in the dynamic interrelationship between the court cards of the tarot.

Each of the sixteen court cards has two elemental properties. One is active and operates in the foreground, while the other is passive and serves as a background for the other element. The passive or background elements of the court cards are derived from the suits. The active or foreground elements are based on the ranks of the court cards. It sounds confusing at first, but it is quite easy to understand.

Wands — Fire
Cups — Water
Swords — Air
Disks — Earth

All Wands have as their general background element Fire. This applies to the number cards as well as to the court cards. When interpreting the number cards, the element of their suit should always be considered. The number cards only have the background suit element, but the court cards have an additional foreground elemental property based on their ranks.

Kings — Fire
Queens — Water
Knights — Air
Knaves — Earth

When you combine these two elemental properties of each court card, they take on sixteen distinct identities that are the sixteen basic human personality types. This is why the court cards are used to stand for human beings in tarot divinations. Everyone falls into one of these sixteen basic types of human personality, as expressed by pairs of elements. The active element derived from the rank is given first, followed by the background element derived from the suit.

King of Wands — Fire of Fire
Queen of Wands — Water of Fire
Knight of Wands — Air of Fire
Knave of Wands — Earth of Fire

King of Cups — Fire of Water
Queen of Cups — Water of Water
Knight of Cups — Air of Water
Knave of Cups — Earth of Water

King of Swords — Fire of Air
Queen of Swords — Water of Air
Knight of Swords — Air of Air
Knave of Swords — Earth of Air

King of Disks — Fire of Earth
Queen of Disks — Water of Earth
Knight of Disks — Air of Earth
Knave of Disks — Earth of Earth

The elemental pairs can be of great use in figuring out how to assign the court cards to individuals by personality type. For example, the King of Wands is all Fire in his nature. His ability to restrain his temper is weak when he is contradicted. He must dominate others and is a natural leader. By contrast, the Queen of Wands is Water acting against a backdrop of Fire. These elements are in opposition, so there is conflict in her nature. Her fiery temperament can sometimes flash with instability, but usually she is able to apply it smoothly, like burning oil.

These are the most important of the Golden Dawn tarot correspondences. They can be of great help in gaining a deeper understanding of the meaning of the cards in divination layouts, and are of value in clarifying a reading that is uncertain or subject to two possible interpretations. Even though the individual correspondences are not printed on the faces of the *Necronomicon Tarot* cards, users of the deck should be aware that the cards were designed to be in harmony with these correspondences. The full power of the Golden Dawn system can be applied when the cards are used.

CHAPTER 4

Trumps

0 Fool: Azathoth (Air)

THE BLIND IDIOT god, Azathoth, sits naked on his throne of carved obsidian, blubbering from the corners of his thick lips as he pipes trilling notes from his reed flute. His misshapen body is covered with filth and of an unhealthy complexion, for it has never felt the sunlight, and his hair hangs matted and uncut over his obese torso. Slime seeps from the hollow sockets of his blind eyes. His face, strangely obscured by uncouth angles that defy comprehension, glows with its own dark inner fire.

Within his hall of shadow, where is to be found no sane geometry but only distortions of space, the music of his flute wraps around his shoulders like a living cloak, which is composed of the transparent bodies of countless intertwined dancing naked sprites both male and female, the spirits of the notes that tremble on the air like crystalline bells. The flute is cracked on its end, so that it can form no perfect note, and for this reason all of these dancing and lustful spirits are imperfect. Some lack a hand or an arm, others a foot or a leg; some are without eyes, others without ears. Their bodies are distorted with insane proportions even as the music is strange on the ear, having no certain modality.

Excrement and slime surround the base of the throne, and in this rest the filthy feet of the god. His great head is cocked to one side, as though listening. His hands are unnaturally large, his fingers long and dexterous as they seek out the sound holes of his instrument. All is dark and gloom-covered except for the cloak of sound, which shines with bright colors as though illuminated from within as it streams away into infinite distance. It resembles a dancing rainbow and contains all the forms and motions of everything that was, is, and will be in the universe.

Upright: innocence, simplicity, naiveté, childlike wonder, spiritual path, new beginning, journey of discovery, higher guidance, need for prudence.

Inverted: credulity, heedlessness, folly, inability to adapt, blindness, good advice ignored, meaningless talk, impulsiveness, rashness, danger ahead.

I Magician: Nyarlathotep (Mercury)

HE STANDS ATOP the crest of a giant sand dune in the Empty Space, his swirling cloak silvered by the light of the waning moon as it billows behind him on the night breeze. All his clothing is black: his cloak, his hooded robe, his tall boots. Within his hood, black silk wraps across his face like the caul that sometimes covers the face of a newborn babe. His body is of human shape, tall and straight. His hands appear gloved, so black is his skin, and his bony fingers are impossibly long. Upon them, jewels set in rings catch the moonlight, imitating the stars in the black vault of heaven above his head.

With his right hand, he points a judgment at a man who kneels in supplication at his feet. The unfortunate man's body is consumed by a wasting magic so that the skin and flesh that cover his bones have turned to dust and blow away on the wind, leaving only the white bones of his skeleton, which have not yet collapsed into a heap upon the sand. With his left hand, Nyarlathotep peels away the lower portion of his black silk caul, revealing part of his face within the oval of his hood. Yet no face is there to expose, for where nose and mouth should be there is only a blackness speckled with the same stars that are behind him in the night sky, so that the illusion is given that his head is hollow and that the stars may be seen through his hood.

A spiritual essence, which glows with eerie green light and resembles a stream of mist, coils up from the desiccated bones of the man who kneels on the sands and flows like an undulating serpent into the hood of the god at the place where his mouth would be, if he possessed a mouth. Nyarlathotep consumes the human essence of the poor fool who displeased him, but whether it is for some strange, incorporeal sustenance or for a darker and more sinister purpose, who can know?

Upright: attainment, mastery, skill, artfulness, strong will, dominant mind, eloquence, persuasiveness, misdirection, manipulation, transformation, a great wonder.

Inverted: craftiness, slyness, deception, leading astray, illusion, a dangerous person, abuse of power, false glamour, hurtful revelation, a trickster, attempt to entrap.

II High Priestess: Bast (Moon)

A SLENDER YOUNG priestess wearing an elaborate mask in the shape of a cat's head that completely covers her head and is supported on her shoulders sits enthroned with her bare feet firmly on the stones of the floor. She is dressed in ancient Egyptian fashion, and her breasts are exposed. Silver ornaments adorn her bare arms and ankles. Her necklace is in the form of a large silver lunar crescent that hangs in the valley of her breasts. In one hand she holds a black ankh by its loop, so that it dangles in front of the arm of her throne, and in the other hand she holds vertically at the side of her chair the white shaft of a lotus wand in the form of an oversized arrow. The flower of the lotus is formed by the expanded plum of multicolor feathers that fletch the inverted arrow, and the lower end of the stem terminates in a silver arrowhead.

Behind her looms the stone statue of the goddess Bast in the shape of a seated Egyptian cat, somewhat resembling the modern Siamese with its slender body and short coat of hair. The statue is enormous, twice the height of a man. It looks forward with a tranquil expression on its face, its green eyes realistically fashioned from jet, jade, and ivory. It is so positioned that it almost appears to be an astral projection of the priestess, a spiritual expression of another side of her identity. Her mask resembles the head of the statue of the goddess.

At the base of the throne upon the polished stones of the temple floor in front of her feet rests a wooden bowl filled with milk. A living Egyptian cat, all black in color, leans down to lap at the milk. Another that is all white rubs its shoulder lovingly against the bare leg of the priestess. Yet another that is gray lies draped across the lap of the priestess, gazing forward alertly so that its head is in line with the head of the statue and the mask of the priestess. The carved paws of a lioness adorn the legs of the throne, the high back of which bears a carving in the shape of the disk of the full moon touched by the waning moon on the left and the waxing moon on the right.

Upright: mystery, wisdom teaching, spiritual secrets, benevolent guide, initiation, opened mind, higher communication, entry into a circle, spiritual gift.

Inverted: dangerous instruction, intrigues, spiritual burden, trust betrayed, oath broken, evil counsel, dark secrets, the wrong path, sterile teachings.

III Empress: Shub-Niggurath (Venus)

THE GODDESS STANDS in the lascivious pose of a dancer, completely naked. Her head is bestial and strange, bristling with wild hair like the black bristles of the boar and having four horns, two that curve upward and two that curve downward on each side. Her ears are pointed and tufted at their tips. The pupils of her wildly glaring eyes are lateral slits like those of a goat, and her snarling mouth is filled with sharp teeth resembling the teeth of a wolf. Voluptuous rounded breasts cover her chest even down to her belly, but her belly is smooth and its outward dome shows that she is pregnant. Her arms are those of a woman, poised gracefully in dance. In one hand she holds a human skull and in the other a noose of twisted cloth with which to strangle her enemies. Her legs and feet are those of a goat, covered with shaggy hair and cloven.

The dancing body of the goddess is enclosed in an aura lit along its edges with flames. The aura has the shape of a pointed oval and resembles a widely gaping vulva. In this flaming portal to other worlds she dances, both framed and sustained by its curved walls. It is most shocking to write that the insides of her hairy thighs are stained with menstrual blood that seeps from her sex, as the vulva of this dark goddess of endless fecundity gapes open.

Her dance is the dance of life and death. Around her feet numerous naked and horned infants lie squawling, or sit and gape, or crawl on hands and knees, or cling to her leg, so that there is no place for her to set down her dancing foot without crushing one of them.

Upright: fertility, vitality, excess of passion, wildness, unchecked enthusiasm, strong growth, good health, womb of nature, pregnancy, new life, maternal instincts, a sensual woman.

Inverted: frenzy, lustfulness, boundaries exceeded, generative excess, mutation, deformity, obsession with flesh, unhealthy growth, possible disease, a kind of stillbirth or abortion that arose from excess.

IV Emperor: Amun (Aries)

WITHIN THE EMBROIDERED and beaded curtains of the sanctuary at the heart of the great temple at Karnack stands the bronze statue of the god Amun, man-sized and naked, his body sheathed in gold leaf so that his well-muscled limbs glow in the flames of the lamps. At the sides of his head curl the horns of the ram, but in every other respect his is human. The life-like figure seems to wait knowingly for the embrace of one of his youthful priestesses, who will soon enter the sanctuary and wrap herself around the statue, her head thrown back in ecstasy as she strives to press within her body his enormous erect phallus. The look of lustful madness that will distort her beautiful Egyptian face makes a strange contrast to the serene and handsome countenance of the god.

A halo of flickering torchlight clothes the body of the naked god. Wisps of steam rise from the gleaming bronze, revealing an inner heat that is awakened by lust. It is clear from its stance that the statue has been shaped for the embraces of its young priestesses. Its shadowed eyes are cunningly fashioned from bits of jet, lapis lazuli, and ivory, so that they appear alive and aware as they gaze deeply into the ecstatic face of the god's lover.

Upright: virility, potency, impregnation, seminal idea, creative spark, first beginnings, masculine force, initial thrust, penetration, determined purpose, passionate man.

Inverted: instability, false start, impractical idea, lack of foundation, wasted force, inertia, heaviness, rigidity of mind, lost opportunity, anxiety, failure to perform, impotence.

V Hierophant: Dagon (Taurus)

SILVERY SCALES COVER the vast naked body of this ruler of the Deep Ones as he emerges from the ocean, bits of kelp clinging to his shining limbs. Like the amphibian he resembles, he appears to be sexless, but this is a deception for his phallus only emerges during his couplings with Shub-Niggurath. He walks upright from the shallows, the weight of the great mass of his head, which is shaped like that of a dolphin and has no neck where it joins his broad shoulders, bowing him down so that his long arms hang almost to the surface of the waves. His fingers are elongated and webbed, even as are his toes that remain concealed by the sea as he takes an enormous stride forward. In the middle of his high forehead is set a single lidless eye, vast and round as the shield of a warrior. He has no ears but only small holes where ears should be, and on the sides of his head gill slits gape and gasp the night air—for he never ventures from the sea except at night.

The glow from the moon plays strangely on his body, which is semi-transparent, as though composed of some jellylike substance. His mouth is a broad slit, his voice when he speaks deeper than the tolling of the greatest bell. He strides forward under moonlight in the shallows, newly emerged from the sea with its waters still streaming from his limbs, calling out to his worshippers who dwell upon the land to approach and bring forth their offerings, for he can approach the shore no closer than the line of the lowest tide.

A nearby lighthouse, its size dwarfed by the mountainous body of the god, casts its golden beam across his head and shoulder, illuminating the full horror of his face that has no trace of humanity despite his humanoid body. Dagon turns his back upon the land, where he can never walk or rule. The low-tide line is an invisible barrier that restrains him. His children, the Deep Ones, emerge from the sea around his legs, their bodies more humanoid yet strangely similar to that of the god. Their dark shadows have an aura of menace that threatens the beach.

Upright: tradition, authority, religion, commandment, code of honor, duty, history, the past, weight of precedent, priest, minister, church, temple, morality, confession.

Inverted: lack of honor, hollow observances, suppression, punishment, sin, inquisition, harsh judgment, onerous duty, required religious rites, lack of forgiveness.

VI Lovers: Deep One & Bride (Gemini)

IN THE GREAT hall of Dagon in Atlantis an elder priest has just joined in marriage a young Deep One and his human bride. The priest, who is still human but in the advanced stages of transformation into a Deep One that those who are of mixed blood always experience in old age, stands upon the altar steps behind them, long altar at his back, a holy book in his hands, his resplendent purple robe of office draped around his no longer quite human body. His vaguely froglike face, tinged a faint blue by the strangeness of his blood, gives him the pallor of a corpse, but corpses are not usually so moist and glistening by candlelight. This elder priest looks on with satisfaction as he finalizes the vows of the living couple.

The lovers stand at the base of the altar steps facing each other, holding hands. The bride is a beautiful young woman with dark hair and a pale complexion. In her gray eyes there is a distant look, as though she is in a kind of trance, yet her lips smile and she gazes up into the eyes of her husband with love. She wears a traditional wedding gown of white and ornate heavy silver jewelry studded with jewels—gifts from her new husband. Upon her head is an elaborate jeweled tiara, better adapted to fit the sloped skull of a great frog than a human head.

The groom has little in his appearance that is human save that he stands upright in the general posture of a man. His head is broad and froglike, his skin blue, his eyes dark and gleaming, his mouth a broad gash with almost no lips, nor is any chin visible, but his head appears to run directly down into his deep chest without the need for a neck. Gill slits are faintly visible in the side where his neck should be. He wears a long black robe of formal design trimmed with silver threads that cover his barrel chest and strangely stunted legs.

He holds his bride's slender hand in blunt fingers that are webbed and show the faintest hint of silver scales on their backs. Upon her finger glitters a costly gold ring set around its sides with diamonds, which he has just placed there. Its size and shape are not quite the same as a ring of human manufacture. His expression as he looks deeply into her eyes is commanding, possessive, and lustful.

Upright: love, relationship, marriage, commitment, heartfelt pledge, union, amorous feelings, shared affection, loving partner, soul mate, trust, devotion.

Inverted: bad match, unhappy affair, false affection, betrayal, seduction, violent desire, adultery, divorce, separation, unrequited love, ill-fated partnership, broken vow.

VII Chariot: Beast of Babylon (Cancer)

IN SIZE THE Beast is like a horse, but its hind legs are longer than its front legs and more massive so that when it stands on all fours, its hindquarters are above the level of its shoulders. All four of its feet are like the talons of a bird of prey. Its long and slender tail is barbed on its tip and black, although the scale-covered body of the Beast is a kind of darkling reddish black, the color of dying embers. The leathern wings that it presently holds expanded on either side of its ridged spine in preparation for flight somewhat resemble the wings of a bat. The Beast feeds itself through a gray beak beneath the cluster of its necks, in shape much like the beak of a hawk. When irritated it lets out a shrill cry but it is incapable of articulate speech.

It is a curious feature of the Beast that it has not one head, but seven—or rather, no head at all, since each of its seven heads grows upon a long neck and forms itself in the span of a few minutes, then quickly melts away and is replaced by another head. All the multitude of forming and dissolving heads are human, their patterns taken from the various human prey the Beast has consumed over the millennia, and indeed the head of every man, women, or child it has ever eaten forms itself upon one of its seven necks from time to time, although some heads come forth more often than others—particularly the small yellow-skinned bald head of Belaka, a necromancer of the East that the Beast ate long ago. Poor Belaka has bad teeth and is troubled by toothache. He is renowned as the wisest head of Babylon, and the Beast is both his prison and his kingdom, for although he can never leave it or control its doings, he has more freedom than any other head to shape himself periodically on one or another of those seven snakelike necks.

When dusk falls, the Beast leaves the sewers beneath the ruins of Babylon through a pit in the ground to hunt its human prey. It stands in the final glow from the western sky, its wings spread and expanding with blood to the great size that will bear it in flight. The creature is highlighted against the red sunset amid the fallen stones of the ancient city, standing beside a pillar broken into three parts that lies close to the pit from which it has just emerged. All of the seven heads are excited at the time of twilight just before it launches itself into the sky. They shout and weep and laugh—except for the head of Belaka, which stares sourly into the distance and broods upon his fate.

Upright: victory, conquest, triumph, rulership, enforcement of authority, commanding, fruits of battle, admiration of the crowd, fame, glory, control over others.

Inverted: vainglorious display, domination, abuse of authority, exacting tribute, consequences of defeat, inflicting humiliation, dictator, tin god, petty tyrant.

VIII Strength: Shoggoth (Leo)

A CREATURE, SIMILAR in form to that of an amoeba but with the size of an elephant, raises upon its back a huge block of black stone, which it intends to fit into place in the unfinished cyclopean wall of some vast construction resembling a fortress that has non-Euclidian geometry. The angles of the wall are difficult to hold in the mind. The wall is being constructed on the heights of a great mountainside so that it seems an extension of the mountain itself. The shoggoth balances the block with its pseudopods, which it extrudes for the purpose.

Bright sparks like stars and cloudy ill-defined shapes are visible within the translucent depths of its amorphous bulk. On the surface of its gelatinous body can arise eyes, mouths, and ears of inhuman and primitive shape. These are not a part of its permanent appearance, but are formed and extended to serve as the sense organs of the creature as a matter of convenience, to enable it to work in its environment. It makes as many or as few as it needs at any given moment. It has no feet or legs but moves across the stones after the manner of a snail or snake, by undulating its lower surface and, as it were, rolling itself forward, for in truth it has no top or bottom.

Its taskmaster, one of the crinoid race of Elder Things that made it, hovers in the air beside the wall on the hummingbirdlike beating of its pale-gray membranous wings, which extend out of the grooves between the flat vertical ridges around the circumference of its barrel-shaped body, wings like curved fans that are hinged at the top and serrated along their edges. Its leathery dark-gray body is dwarfed by the shoggoth in the way a man is dwarfed by an elephant. From the midpoint on the ridges between its wings, which somewhat resemble the staves of a barrel, extend appendages like arms that branch into five parts, each of which subdivides into five small tips like fingers. Each of the five vertical ridges has its appendage, but four are folded up close to the creature's body. The fifth arm of this crinoid master wields a whip that glows along its length with electrical fire. With this instrument it lashes the shoggoth on to greater efforts.

The yellowish head of this crinoid creature is shaped like a starfish and sits flat on a thick neck of a light-gray color that extends up from the tapered top of the barrel-shaped body of the being. The head is fleshy and covered all over with rainbow-hued cilia, and has at its top a slit for breathing. At the end of each point of the starfish-head is a short yellow stalk with a red eye on its tip. Between the points of the head extend trumpet-shaped mouths with sharp teeth. At the tapered base of the creature's body, five thick gray flexible branching appendages serve as legs, each terminating in a triangular foot. These are drawn up while the creature is in flight.

The shoggoth reacts to the agony of the whip by forming on its back multiple eyestalks that resemble those of its crinoid masters, with which it glares at the flying being that torments it. It longs to lash out with its pseudopods and kill its tormentor, which it could easily do, but the mind control of the Elder Thing restrains it, though without possessing the power to entirely subdue its rebellious rage.

Upright: indomitable spirit, harnessed force, endurance, perseverance, directed energy, refusal to surrender, defiance, passive resistance, purposefulness, valor, nobility.

Inverted: brute strength, frustration, smoldering rage, resentment, potential for violence, unbridled anger, loss of control, ungovernable, lashing out, misuse of force, bullying.

IX Hermit: I'thakuah (Virgo)

MORE ANCIENT THAN the oldest trees, almost as old as the stone walls that surround her, the witch I'thakuah waits and listens within the sunless cisterns beneath the ruins of the city of Irem, gathering information from the dwellers in the deeps for her lord Nyarlathotep. The weight of years has bent her body and hunched her back so that at times her hooked nose almost touches the ground at her feet. Naked save for a filthy cloak of wool that wraps around her shoulders, her gray hair hangs wild and half obscures her ancient face, which is twisted with an expression of malicious glee by whatever fire of madness burns in her heart. Her legs are bent and of no great length, but her shoulders and arms are massively muscled and of unnatural size, so that her hands are like the hands of a giant. The black nails on the ends of her fingers almost resemble claws. She sits before her fire on a ledge of rock within the great dry cistern, contemplating her face in an oval mirror of polished silver with the vanity of a young girl. Tiny black eyes glitter in the wrinkled depths of her face, and her lips writhe away from blackened toothless gums as she mumbles obscene words in a lost tongue. Behind her rears a pyramid of human skulls. The skull on top is still reddened with dried blood, where its skin has been peeled away.

Upright: wisdom, secrets revealed, a teacher, discipline, study, testing, examination, asceticism, denial of the flesh, mind over matter, chastity, commitment, vocation, dedication to a purpose, self-denial, spiritualized sexuality.

Inverted: intolerance, fanaticism, self-abuse, narrow-thinking, rigidity of belief, knowledge withheld, loss of faith, lack of guidance, vital energy squandered, ignorance.

X Wheel: Yog-Sothoth (Jupiter)

THE NIGHT SKY above the ancient megaliths of Stonehenge is lit by the colors of the coming of this lord of portals, who is gatekeeper and ruler of all going in and coming out not only in this world, but in the farthest reaches of time and space. Only his face appears in the heavens, for body he has none, and his face is an abstraction of various sizes of translucent glowing colored spheres that intersect and turn at different rates against the backdrop of a great inverted triangle of light, so that the spheres seem to define in some strange and misshapen way the features of an enormous but utterly inhuman countenance that is somewhat akin to the Arikh Anpin, the Vast Countenance of the Kabbalists; and indeed it was Yog-Sothoth who inspired this myth. It is the face of Shaddai, the Almighty, that none may look upon lest they be blasted by its power.

The face of the god shines above a beam of light that rises from the recumbent altar stone of Stonehenge, where a naked youth has been sacrificed with a stone blade by the linen-robed high priest of the cult of Yog-Sothoth worshippers. About the face of the god there is the beginning of a vortex that forms in the night sky as he opens the way between worlds. The stones of the circle glow with power.

Upright: change, transformation, turn of fortune, good luck, a way opens, moving onward, progress, evolution, act of fate, milestone, opportunity for advancement.

Inverted: inversion of situation, bad luck, turn for the worse, a way closes, obstruction, stumbling block, setback, lack of progress, changelessness, treading water, lost opportunity.

XI Justice: Spawn in Sphere (Libra)

IN A VAULTED chamber deep beneath the earth hangs a massive cage of iron formed from interlocking bands riveted where they overlap to form a sphere. The cage is sustained in the air in the center of the chamber by three iron chains that dangle from the concentric rings of ancient stones that form the inverted bowl that is the ceiling of the vault. Each link of these chains is large enough for a man to pass his hand through, could he reach it, but the iron sphere hangs higher above the flagstone floor than a tall man can reach. Flames burn in brackets around the circle of the wall, giving a good illumination of the thing that crouches within its iron prison, but the mind revolts from its alien shape and at first refuses to perceive it. The cage appears to be filled only with a smoky translucent mass, like a polished irregular lump of rock crystal, were it possible that any crystal so large might be found in the earth.

It is only when the thing moves that an observer is able to notice it, and then it is perceived to be a creature of roughly humanoid shape, having a head, two arms, and two legs—but there the resemblance stops. The proportions of its limbs are distorted, the arms too long, the clawed fingers of the hands too large, talons like those of a hawk where its feet should be, its head a mass of snaky ropes or tentacles that rises from its shoulders without the support of a neck. Its head is as massive as that of an elephant, with a score of slender trunks that writhe like serpents. In shape its head may be likened to the body of a deep-sea-dwelling cephalopod. Each elongated side, soft and pulsing on the boneless crown, bears three tiny black eyes that resemble the eyes of an insect. Along its hunched back are folded great membranous wings, cruelly compressed by the iron bands of its prison, which is scarcely large enough in circumference to contain it bulk.

As its shape becomes known to the mind in parts and pieces, it is perceived to be a perfect miniature copy of the warrior lord of the Old Ones, mighty Cthulhu, and can only be one of his soldier spawn created countless aeons ago to fight against the Elder Things and their dread servants, the shoggoths. A few of the spawn of Cthulhu survive deep beneath the earth in caverns having no exits to the surface, for these creatures are eternal and endure without nourishment, weakened by their fast but deathless. Cut off from the mind control of their maker, who lies dreaming beneath the sea in the sunken city of R'lyeh, they are left to their own resources, and can do no more than watch and wait and plan for the awakening of their dread lord.

How this spawn came to be drawn up from the bowels of the earth and imprisoned in the vault, which has but a single small archway to provide entrance to the monks who study it, remains a mystery.

It is bound not merely by its massive riveted iron bands, but by potent sigils of dark necromancy upon the stones of the walls and ceiling of the vault at intervals. Were these pentacles to be effaced, the iron cage would not hold the spawn of Cthulhu for an instant, but their secret power reinforces the black iron and renders it unbreakable. So has the creature hung and waited through the centuries. The warrior monks of the monastery above the vault serve as its warders, but the monks did not bind it here, for they have no such great skill in magic. Those who built the vault and made the spawn their prisoner have passed to dust and been forgotten in time. Only the spawn remains, and it does not speak about those who bound it.

Upright: balanced use of force, weighing of factors, fair decision, judicious authority, necessary adjustment, a wrong righted, truth revealed, impartial hearing.

Inverted: prejudiced decision, lack of judgment, imbalance, favoritism, bribery, perversion of justice, legal delay, a decision postponed, suspension, unfair decision.

XII Hanged Man: Well of the Seraph (Water)

HALF BURIED IN the silt within the depths of an ancient desert well, its walls lined with crumbling stone blocks, resides a wooden chest sheathed all over its sides and ornate lid with gold leaf. Rings of metallic gold project from its sides, evidently intended for the insertion of poles that would allow the chest to be carried between two men. Upon the lid of this chest crouch two golden angelic figures that face each other, their wings arching over their heads so that the wingtips nearly touch, as though to shield the chest. A strange glow fills the water, making the sides of the chest shine.

From behind this golden box a spiritual creature that is shaped like a legless dragon or serpent undulates through the glowing water around the perimeter of the well, its insubstantial body a column of fire.

The face of the thing is human and beautiful, but so androgynous that it is difficult to tell whether it is the face of a man or of a woman. It wears a serene expression of implacable judgment that is without mercy. So long is its body that the waters of the well appear filled with its form, which crosses and recrosses over its own length in a bewildering way, making it difficult to tell where it begins or ends.

An Arab nomad, stripped naked to the waist and barefoot, wearing only loose cotton trousers, struggles in the deep water as the guardian of the well wraps its golden coils around his chest and limbs, raising its inhumanly beautiful face to stare into his terror-stricken eyes. Although the spiritual creature is able to hinder his movements, its body is insubstantial to his touch, and he is unable to effectively grasp it or thrust it away. From the mud at the bottom of the well project human bones, testifying that other imprudent treasure seekers have met the fate that awaits the nomad.

Upright: suspension, waiting, need for patience, delay, willing sacrifice, trial of endurance, test of faith, mystery.

Inverted: abandonment, despair, involuntary suffering, frustration, opposition, hands tied, act of fate, humiliation, powerlessness, accident on water, overwhelmed.

XIII Death: Tsathoggua (Scorpio)

IN A STEAMING jungle swamp, beneath the moss-covered creepers of vast trees of primordial age, beside a stinking slime-encrusted pond of dark water, rests a statue of polished black stone that has the shape of a seated frog with the head of a man. It is slightly larger than human-sized, and the hands of the monster are in the shape of human hands. It seems to leer down from its podium at the spectacle of horror in the clearing at its base.

A naked man kneels on the ground, arms bound together and elevated behind his back on rope attached to an iron ring high on the side of a thick post, so that he is compelled to lean forward toward the effigy of the god as though in unwilling worship. Strips of skin have been torn from his arms, chest, and thighs, and his belly gapes open, spilling forth a mass of his intestines that have spread a pool of drying blood around his knees. This would be horrible enough, for through some evil magic the human sacrifice still lives, were it not that he is also missing his face, which has been torn away from his skull as though it were a mask. His lidless eyes stare through a veil of blood, and his exposed and lipless teeth part to express a horror that is deeper than could be provoked by any agony, no matter how terrible.

Before the squat statue of the pitiless god of the swamps stands an ornately carved stone pillar supporting a heavy brass bowl of strange design. The pillar is short, no taller than the waist of a standing man. The bowl is filled with a noxious black ichor having deep red highlights in the torchlight. Its surface ripples and thrusts upward a liquid pseudopod that quests forward through the night air toward the unfortunate captive at the stake as though somehow smelling his blood, for it has no eyes with which to see its way. Perhaps the carven eyes of Tsathoggua

are its guide. It extends its way toward the faceless man like a hungry infant that blindly seeks a milk-filled breast upon which to feed.

Upright: transformation, rebirth, transition, pilgrimage, ordeal, risen from the ashes, a new identity.

Inverted: dark night of the soul, terror, failure of faith, spiritual emptiness, surrender to physical urges, loss of direction, a death.

XIV Temperance: Reanimators (Sagittarius)

IN A WORKSHOP beneath the Sphinx of Egypt, reanimators of the secret Order of the Sphinx rend down the ancient mummy of a pharaoh into its essential salts in preparation for the reanimation of the corpse. A male servant in a white linen skirt and leather slippers, head shaved and torso bare, gently lowers the desiccated arm of the mummy into an enormous copper kettle that rests on an iron frame over a charcoal fire in an iron fireplace on the open floor of the chamber. The arm slides into greenish liquid that bubbles noxiously, sending up fumes that pass out from the chamber through a vent in its stone ceiling. Other severed portions of the mummy are distinguishable heaped in a wheeled bin from which the arm has been taken. A dark-haired female servant robed discreetly in plain linen uses a long wooden ladle to stir the contents of the kettle.

In the background, a member of the Order of the Sphinx stands beside a wall-mounted oil torch. He is dressed to resemble Nyarlathotep, his god, in a long black robe with a hood, his features concealed behind a black silk scarf that covers his face like a caul. He holds up a cylinder of transparent green glass to the light of the torch, studying the powder that almost fills this bottle, which is sealed with a stopper of lead.

Upright: refinement, purification, renewal, blending of opposites, health, the golden mean, harmony, perfecting of worth.

Inverted: dilution, weakening, confusion, intemperance, corruption, toxicity, spoiling, fatal imperfection.

XV Devil: Cthulhu (Capricorn)

THE SUBMERGED ISLAND of Cthulhu has risen above the surface of the southern ocean, as it does at rare intervals when the stars in their turnings come aright. The waves wash at the slime-covered, kelp-draped stone blocks of the city of R'lyeh, newly ascended from their watery rest. Chief among them is an enormous obelisk of black stone, as tall as a modern skyscraper, of unnatural thickness and uncouth geometry, so that none of its angles are right angles, and it seems thicker at the sloped top than at its base. Other lesser blocks lie scattered in the muck and ooze of the island, at first glance disordered, but upon closer examination the roofs of massive buildings.

Near the base of the black obelisk, the bronze doors in a portal in a sloped face of stone gape wide as through thrown open by some massive force. Emerged from the darkness within stands mighty Cthulhu, newly wakened from his sleep of dreaming death. The god has stepped forth from the doorway on thick legs that are as yet only partially formed, for the body of the god is not solid flesh but composed of vapors that he gathers in from the air and sea around him, giving him a gelatinous appearance of green and blue. His great clawed hand that reaches out is well-shaped, as are his head, torso, and folded wings. He resembles the spawn held prisoner in the iron sphere, but on a much more massive scale. The black obelisk is like a mountain, yet it fails to dwarf the body of great Cthulhu. Sea birds, no more than tiny dots, circle around his tentacled head with its six glaring eyes, so like the eyes of a spider in their inverted triangular patterns.

In the roiling waves that wash over his striding legs, a freighter makes haste to steam away from the island, bearing the surviving members of its crew unlucky enough to have walked on risen R'lyeh. They do not dare to confront the creature of nightmare they have accidentally released by breaking the seal on the bronze doors that held him captive in his tomb. Cthulhu makes his ponderous way toward the ship, which can scarcely hope to escape before he crushes it in his grasp.

In the deep blue of the early morning sky, the rising sun is a part of the unseen alignment of the heavens that allowed the island of sunken R'lyeh to rise and Cthulhu to wake from his deathlike sleep.

Upright: defiance of authority, rebellion, animal vitality, brute strength, lustfulness, personal magnetism, dominance, reckless courage, willfulness, arrogance, pride.

Inverted: malice, resentment, betrayal, oath-breaking, anger, abuse of power, intimidation of others, bullying, deliberate cruelty, forbidden forms of sexuality, pleasure in wickedness.

XVI Tower: Great Ziggurat (Mars)

THE FABLED TOWER of Babel rises in the form of a
great ziggurat, or stepped pyramid, of seven levels. It
occupies a plain beside the river Euphrates. The ziggurat is surrounded by a great congregation of people.
On the top of the ziggurat a devotional fire burns on
an altar. Richly robed priests are in the midst of con-
ducting a ceremony that is directed at the fire, within
the flames of which opens an oval portal, an occult
gateway to another time and place. A vast beam of
light extends upward from the fire on the altar like
the beam of a searchlight, piercing the heavens themselves, which are troubled by roiling storm clouds.

In reaction to this ascending beam, a bolt of lightning of unnatural size and strength strikes downward
to split the top of the ziggurat and fracture its body
with a gaping fissure, so that the priests in the midst
of their worship are thrown outward and burned by

the flash of the lightning, and begun to tumble off from its rumblings. Fire rains down on the dismayed worshippers surrounding the ziggurat, causing them to cower in terror and throw their arms up in a hopeless effort to shield themselves.

Upright: grand scheme, edifice, monument, ambitious plan, construction, social elevation, fame, glory, honors, great church or temple, skyscraper, mansion.

Inverted: white elephant, boondoggle, collapse of plan, destruction of property, disaster, fire, loss due to conflict, social humiliation, infamy, dishonor, a disease.

XVII Star: Ishtar (Aquarius)

A BEAUTIFUL YOUNG woman with long dark hair, in which is set a golden diadem bearing a single large sapphire, stands naked beneath the night sky at the margin of the River Tigris. On the far bank of the river grow tall grasses. Her bare feet leave prints in their approach through the soft mud. She strains forward and upward with one hand toward the bright star Sirius, the Dog Star, that shines above the river, so that her slender fingers seem about to pluck the star out of the heavens. Her leading foot, upon which she balances, is partially beneath the surface of the water, but her other foot is dry upon the bank.

Beside her, keeping a vigilant guard, stands a large male hunting hound, its intelligent eyes staring outward, as though it has just heard some sound with its sharp ears. It strains its lean and muscular body forward as though eager to attack. She remains oblivious to the danger, secure in the power of her protector.

Rising from the horizon on the Mesopotamian plain behind her is the silhouette of a ziggurat. Above it blazes the star Venus, which is brighter than the star Sirius and lower in the sky. Venus almost appears to crown the ziggurat with its resplendent rays, even as the sapphire on her diadem crowns the lady. Other bright stars dot the heavens, but none of them can compare to these two great lights.

Upright: hope, divine gift, cleansing of the soul, renewal of purpose, destiny, guiding light, a wish granted, guardian angel.

Inverted: hope delayed, a setback, minor misfortune, need for patience, reassessment, an error, a dry spell, overtaxing resources.

XVIII Moon: Hounds of Leng (Pisces)

ON OPPOSITE SIDES of a rough path that extends through the tall grasses of the windswept plateau of Leng, two enormous dogs sit partially concealed by the grasses, waiting for a hapless traveler to pass between them. In general shape the dogs are similar to mastiffs, having heavy shoulders and thick necks, upon which are mounted blunt and massively muscled jaws filled with sharp teeth. The dogs pant and slaver in the dim morning light, which has caused a pale silver mist that wets the grasses and hangs close to the path. There is a madness in their staring eyes, as though each can scarcely restrain itself from vaulting forward to tear at the throat of unseen prey. At their feet grow toadstools, some of which show signs of having been broken off and gnawed.

The silver crescent of the waning moon hangs low in the eastern predawn sky, which begins to pale near the horizon. In the air above the place on the horizon where the path seems to lead floats the extraordinary mirage of a great and alien city. It almost seems to rise up from the landscape, and might be mistaken for a real city were it not so pallid and translucent. Its towering buildings are of inhuman design, strangely massive and uncouth, some of them thicker at their flat tops than at their bases, and composed of chaotic angles. Walkways that lack protective guardrails span the spaces from building to building at various levels.

There is a general aura of hidden menace about this scene, as though the dangers that lie concealed in the shadows of the tall grasses may be greater than the obvious threat of the waiting wild dogs.

Upright: illusion, sterility, danger on the path, hostile environment, traps, pitfalls, hidden enemies, deception, lies, concealment, need for caution.

Inverted: nightmares, insanity, irrational fears, obsession, phobia, emotional chaos, brewing evil, poison, black magic, slanders, hatred.

XIX Sun: The Empty Space (Sun)

THE PITILESS SUN blazes down with unending fury upon the rolling sand dunes of the vast desert known as the Empty Space. Each pale-pink dune is like a great frozen wave of sand that towers forty feet or more. Rising heat makes the air above the dunes shimmer and gives them a wet appearance. Along the slope of one of the dunes whirls the column of a dust devil. It undulates into the sky, carrying streamers of dust and sand with it. Low hills of reddish stone line the horizon.

Within the body of the dust devil an inhuman face is dimly visible. The face is difficult to perceive in the ever-changing column of sand because its parts are insubstantial and disassociated from each other. The widely separated eyes tilt at unnatural angles, the mouth gapes as though screaming. Perhaps the face expresses the chaotic identity of the whirlwind itself; or perhaps it is the tortured soul of some unfortunate travel on the desert who has been caught up in its turnings.

The tiny figure of a lone rider on a camel is visible galloping away from the dust devil. The rider wears the garb of a Bedouin. He turns to look over his shoulder as he lashes the rump of the camel with his whip. It is uncertain whether he will escape its pursuit. The parts of the face within its tuning column regard him with hunger. In the distance is a green oasis of palm trees and sparkling water, the safe haven of the harried desert nomad, should he be able to reach it in time.

Upright: higher power, natural law, vital warmth, revelation, clarity, greatness, purification, self-awareness, essential truth, the center, heart of the matter, stripping away shadows, something of value, wealth.

Inverted: burning of superfluous material, withering away of excess, pitiless exposure of essentials, crisis of personal identity, a force of nature, impersonal ordeal, period of difficulties.

XX Judgement: Guardian of Eden (Fire)

A BROOK RUNS between deep banks through a grassy meadow. On each side of the brook are low rounded hills, rising like the breasts of the earth. On the crest of the low hill on the left side of the stream stand the naked skeleton of a great tree that has been dead for so long its wooden bones are bare of bark and show their weathered whiteness. On the crest of the opposite hill grows a flourishing tree covered with green leaves, the boughs of which hang heavy with ripe red fruit that resemble rounded pears.

Spanning the brook is an arched stone bridge with low walls. Built into the middle of the bridge there is an elaborate stone seat with a high carved back that faces in the same direction as the flow of the stream, so that anyone who sits upon the seat finds himself looking across the bridge toward the east. The back interior of the seat has a strange medusalike face carved into it that has only a single eye in the center of its forehead. The eye is represented by an unfaceted ruby the size of an egg that glows red when struck by the morning sunlight.

Above the brook, the blue sky of day is rent or torn like a sheet, so that the stars of night shine through the gap, which has just given passage to a terrifying angelic being that has the face and body of a beautiful woman. In her forehead there is only a single enormous eye that has a uniform blackness over its surface. Her lips writhe away from her teeth in an expression of fury. Her hair radiates around her head in a thousand translucent rainbow streamers that seem to float on the air the way seaweed floats on the currents of the ocean. From her body a thousand translucent arms extend like serpents, all spreading out in a halo around her that half fills the heavens. Droplets of fire rain from these innumerable appendages. They fall from the sky and ignite the grass of the meadow wherever they touch it.

A naked man on the left side of the brook tries to ward off the rain of fire, the expression on his upturned face a mingling of dismay and anguish. He reaches out toward a naked woman on the opposite bank, who cowers to cover her nude body while shielding her head with her hands from the burning droplets of flame.

Upright: reward for honor, favorable ruling, acquittal, proof of innocence, just desserts, impartial decision, elevation of rank or status, restoration, wrong righted.

Inverted: punishment for dishonor, wrath of higher power, retribution, reaping what was sowed, eye for an eye, finding of guilt, harsh justice, full penalty assessed.

XXI World: Yig (Saturn)

A GREAT SERPENT coils in three and one-half turns up the sides of a vast black egg that stands vertically on its larger end. The direction of the snake's sliding body in its ascent is widdershins—against the course of the sun. Its eye is amber flecked with gold, having a vertical pupil. Heat pits are visible along the side of its jaw, which gapes to reveal numerous curved teeth. The head of the snake is adorned by a feathered crest along its top and a ruff of feathers around its neck, giving it a strange appearance. The scales of its body are iridescent and every color of the rainbow. They show a pattern similar to that of a reticulate python.

The feathered snake rears its head straight upward as if to bite the sky. The background above, below, and on either side of the egg is dark and chaotic, filled with storm clouds that are lit from behind by concealed flashes of lightning. The egg and the serpent seem to float in this chaotic void. Directly behind the head of the snake is a vortex in the chaos that swirls the clouds in a spiral that turns clockwise as it focuses inward upon its center, which is located directly behind the jaws of the serpent. The vortex acts as a sort of halo for the serpent's head—its swirling lit by fire against the darker brooding backdrop of the clouds.

The egg is smooth and of a beautiful black tinged with blue, like the night sky. Sparks of light lie scattered across its polished surface. These sparks are stars. Here and there a tiny galaxy is visible. The egg is the universe of creation. The dark clouds are formless chaos, from which the world arose, and upon which it floats like a sealed ark upon the stormy waters of the ocean. The serpent god ascends from the universe, which it encompasses in its coils, to the primal swirling vortex from which all creation descended upon the lightning. Were it to tighten its coils around the universe, the egg of creation would shatter into myriad fragments that could never be reformed.

Upright: fulfillment, completion, totality, summing up, the conclusion of a work, coming full circle, seeing the big picture, final act, last thing to be done.

Inverted: going in circles, sense of futility, lack of comprehension, failure to understand, what goes around comes around, pawn of fate, puppet on a string, something uncompleted.

Wands

Lord — Lady — Commander — Overseer

Predominant color: shades of red

CHAPTER 5

✦

Court Cards

✦

King of Wands: Lord

A LORDLY BEARDED man of middle years, whose long blond hair is restrained by a golden circlet, stands beside an elaborate gilded throne. The snarling heads of lions adorn both arms of the throne, while on the corners of its high back are the heads of eagles. The throne has a red velvet cushion for a seat. Its back legs resemble lion paws, while its front legs are in the shape of eagle talons that grip crystal spheres. The man is dressed in a red tunic embroidered with gold thread, over which is a gilded ceremonial breastplate trimmed with silver. Golden greaves inlaid with silver protect his shins above his leather sandals. Around his neck on a chain hangs a pendant in the shape of an upright triangle of ruby.

The throne occupies a raised marble dais out of doors. Behind it on either side are two translucent pillars of rock crystal, one rose-hued and the other milky white, between which hangs a tall red banner emblazoned in red and gold with a rearing winged lion having two heads, that of a lion and an eagle. On one side of this banner, tall sea cliffs are visible at the base of which break white waves, and on the other side, a galley sails upon the sea beneath the brilliant globe of the sun, shining with painful brightness in the blue sky.

The lord stands stiffly with his left hand on the back of the empty throne, his expression grim as though in the act of passing judgment, and lowers in his right hand a massive black staff that is tipped with a crystal faceted in the shape of a tetrahedron (regular geometric body with four sides, i.e. a three-sided pyramid) toward someone who kneels unseen before the throne, out of the frame of the card. He holds the wand lowered and from its crystal pours forth a blazing ray of radiant energy resplendent with many colors that expands as it extends from the wand. The brightness of the crystal seems to derive its heat and energy from the rays of the sun behind the lord, magnifying and transforming their warmth into a deadly yet beautiful force of destruction.

Upright: Mature man who is impulsive, forceful, generous but also capricious, quick to extend his favor but impatient of delays and furious when contradicted. His impatience can lead him into rash actions he later regrets, but he cannot bear to admit his errors. Anger comes and goes with equal swiftness.

Inverted: Mature man who is overbearing and at times brutal, unable to control his temper, vindictive toward those who oppose him. All his force is in his first attempt, but if this fails he begins to war with himself and loses his purpose. His nature is noble but he corrupts it with his need to always be in control.

Queen of Wands: Lady

A NOBLEWOMAN DRESSED in a long green gown, with a red travel cape trimmed in ermine hanging from her broad shoulders, stands upon the grassy windblown edge of a precipice that overlooks the ocean. She has long red hair and blue eyes, high cheekbones, slender yet muscular limbs, and an upright posture. Her expression is serene, with a trace of arrogance. Upon the front of her gown is embroidered in gold the crest of a winged lion with two heads, that of a lion and an eagle. Around her neck on a chain hangs a pendant in the shape of an inverted triangle of sapphire.

In her left hand she holds the upright shaft of an ebony walking staff that is headed with a large crystal in the shape of a trapezohedron, having twelve sides. Her right hand and wrist are covered in the thick leather of a falconer's glove, which she raises and extends to launch her hunting eagle, in the act of spreading its wings as it leaps into the air from her hand toward its unseen prey. The clouds rolling in the windy sky are lit beneath with the rust and gold of the setting sun. Distant soaring birds fly among them.

Upright: A mature woman with an innate authority over others, deep inner strength of will, relaxed self-assurance, a complete absence of uncertainty, and a sustained sense of purpose that adapts flexibly to achieve its ends. She is well liked by those she dominates, because she does it with such grace and skill, projecting an aura of stability and security.

Inverted: A mature woman whose pride and vanity causes her to believe that she is always right. She obstinately persists in actions even when they are shown to be not in her own best interests, merely from a determination to see them through to the end. She perceives those who disagree with her as her enemies and can become vengeful toward them if they refuse to submit to her will.

Knight of Wands: Commander

A FIERCE YOUNG nobleman in light combat armor made from black iron inlaid with gold and silver wire stands in a chariot, a look of battle lust distorting his handsome aristocratic features. His long auburn hair streams on the rushing wind away from his forward-seeking gray eyes. From his broad shoulders a red cloak lifts and ripples behind him. The crest of a winged lion with two heads, that of a lion and an eagle, ornaments his black breastplate. Around his neck on a chain hangs a pendant in the shape of an upright triangle of yellow topaz.

The warrior stands in a black racing chariot that is drawn by two enormous saber-toothed tigers, their jaws gaping and their dagger like fangs exposed by their snarls. A red copper plaque in the shape of outspread eagle wings, between which is the snarling head of a lion, decorates the front of the chariot.

In his right hand the warrior holds the reins that guide the beasts. In his left hand he levels a black staff with a large crystal on its tip that has the shape of an octahedron (regular geometric body with eight sides). From the crystal, bright multicolored rays of destruction pour forth upon the unseen army of his foes as he races into their midst. There is a wild joy in his eyes, a kind of killing lust that is mirrored in the fierce glares of the saber-toothed cats. The chariot races along the margin of a broad sandy beach upon which break the waves of the sea, foaming with white water.

Upright: A young man who is hasty and rash, who acts quickly without thinking, sometimes in violent ways. His temper is explosive, and when it erupts it scorches anyone who is near. If he does not immediately act, he falls into an indecisive state of mind that paralyzes him because it makes him see both sides of the question equally, until at last he seizes on some unconsidered course merely to free himself from doubt.

Inverted: A young man who enjoys argument for its own sake, merely to contradict others. He is restless and filled with nervous energy, yet unwilling to apply himself to any steady work. He tends to be boastful and a bit of a showoff, but beneath his bold mask he is prey to sudden intense fears and doubts. He can be impatient and even cruel toward others, and may humiliate them with insults and words of contempt. He shows no mercy toward those he attacks.

Knave of Wands: Overseer

AN ATHLETIC, MASCULINE-LOOKING young woman, red hair cut severely short in military fashion, stands beside a narrow upright cage of black iron bars. She holds the door of the cage open with her right hand. In her left hand she cradles a heavy mace that is tipped with a large crystal in the shape of a cube (regular geometric body with six sides). She wears a halter top of black leather that defines her full breasts, and loose red trousers. Her enormous belt buckle is brass cast in the form of a snarling lion's head with eagle's wings on either side.

Around her neck hangs a pendant in the shape of an inverted triangle of emerald. Her eyes are dark gray in color, almost charcoal. Her expression shows brutality mingled with satisfaction. Traces of blood are evident on the cubic head of her mace. Beside the cage is a whipping post from which dangle iron shackles caked with dried blood. A grinning hyena, ignored by the overseer, crouches and sniffs at blood pooled on the ground, its tongue extended. It wears a spiked collar around its neck.

Upright: A young woman or a child who loves to be in control of others, possessing great physical courage, who is ambitious and forceful, refusing to be dissuaded or placated when in pursuit of her goal. Her intense energy gives her a superficial fascination that is apt to be mistaken for beauty. She has a love for power.

Inverted: A young woman or a child given to theatrical displays and tantrums as a way of manipulating others. She tends to be shallow and emotionally unstable, a bit of a bully in getting her own way. Her instability and moodiness make her unreliable, and she cannot be depended on to do what she promised, even though at the time she made the promise, she believed what she said.

Cups

Priest — Priestess — Monk — Scribe

Predominant color: shades of blue

King of Cups: Priest

A SHAVEN-HEADED EGYPTIAN priest in a white linen robe with voluminous sleeves stands behind a carved stone altar table that bears an elaborate silver chalice. He is tall and straight in body, but his face is lined with years. With his left hand he squeezes a bunch of red grapes so that the juice drips and runs between his fingers and falls into the bowl of the chalice, which is almost filled with red grape juice that resembles a kind of transparent blood. With his right hand he makes a pagan gesture of blessing over the chalice. The fingernails on his large hands are trimmed into points, somewhat resembling the claws of a cat. On his feet, unseen behind the altar, he wears simple slippers of white leather. A pendant having the shape of an upright triangle that is made from ruby hangs on a chain around his neck.

Behind his head is a round window through which streams moonlight upon the chalice and the altar. The alter table is supported by four seated stone cats, very tall and slender, which form the legs of the table and face in four directions away from the table. A white linen cloth hangs over the center of the table. On its side is the symbol of the mandorla (an upright oval pointed on both ends) outlined in silver and colored deep blue. The beam of moonlight from the window makes the chalice shine as though illuminated from within.

Upright: A mature man who is sensitive and suggestible, graceful in his manner, easily led by others, willing to follow but unwilling to lead. He is infected by the enthusiasm around him, and energized by it, so that he thinks it is his own, but when removed from it his enthusiasm quickly dies. His nature is inher-ently artistic, expressing itself more in appreciation than creation.

Inverted: A mature man who is easily led into foolish, or even criminal, actions. He is passively sensual and enjoys being aroused by others. He lies merely to avoid unpleasantness or difficulty. Left to his own devices he seldom gets into trouble, but when he falls in with a bad crowd the results can be disastrous. Evil holds an attractive fascination for him.

Queen of Cups: Priestess

A BEAUTIFUL PRIESTESS of Bast, tall and slender, stands behind a wooden table in a kitchen, wearing a simple white linen robe, her dark hair restrained beneath an Egyptian nemyss of white linen. Over the swell of her breasts is tied a long apron of beige cotton. She pours milk from a womb-shaped vase of red clay into a large wooden mixing bowl that is half filled with flour and eggs. Her fingernails are trimmed into points, like the claws of a cat. Affixed to the side of the vase is the symbol of the mandorla, colored blue and edged with silver. Broken eggshells lie on the wooden table beside the bowl. Next to them is a wooden board upon which is a kneaded bun of fresh bread, waiting to be placed in the oven that burns in the masonry wall behind her. Around her neck on a chain hangs a pendant in the shape of an inverted blue triangle made of sapphire.

Upright: A mature woman of a dreamy, inward-looking nature, lost amid her thoughts and memories. She seems to have no personality of her own, but reflects the moods of those around her. She dislikes having her tranquility disturbed by the problems of other human beings and does her best to avoid those who are in difficulty or emotional pain. At the same time, she likes to present a superficial appearance of interest in the affairs of others. She is kind but avoids involvement to protect her own feelings.

Inverted: A mature woman who is shallow, brittle, and vain about her appearance, who cares only about her own ease and the satisfaction of her passing whims. She delights to be the object of attention, to be fashionable and stylish, to be in the vanguard of social trends and have others talking about her and following her around. Even so, she has no firm opinions of her own, but says anything that she thinks will make the strongest impression. Lacking a direction of her own, she is easily led into foolish or petty actions by others.

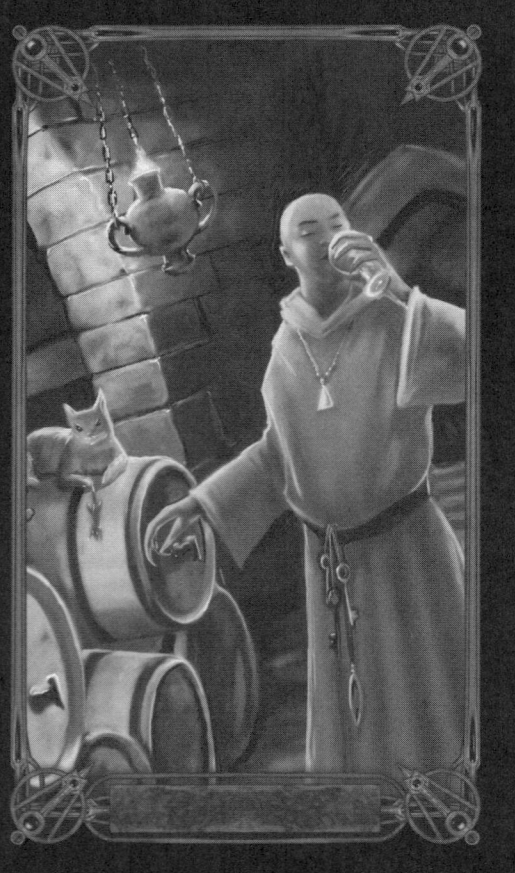

Knight of Cups: Monk

A SOMEWHAT CHERUBIC monk of Bast with clear blue eyes stands in an off-white and soiled linen robe in a wine cellar beside a row of wooden barrels that lie on their sides in a rack along one of the stone walls of the cellar. His head has been shaved but his hair has begun to grow back and covers his scalp with fine stubble. The flame of a brass oil lamp, hanging from the ceiling on three chains, provides illumination for the monk as he samples with thick lips the new wine he has just drawn from one of the barrels. His right hand still rests on the tap of the barrel, while with his left he elevates a glass goblet trimmed with silver to his lips, an expression of joyful contentment on his chubby face as he drinks. The lamplight shines through the wine and gives it the look of transparent blood. His fingernails are pointed, like the claws of a cat.

Hanging from his ropelike sash on a chain are three large keys: one of silver, one of gold, and the third of black iron. The fob of the key chain, which is tucked through his sash and hangs down beside the keys, is a large silver pendant in the shape of a mandorla, enameled over its surface with blue. Around the monk's neck hangs on a chain a pendant in the shape of an upright triangle that is made of yellow topaz. Behind the monk, on top of one of the barrels, a well-fed Egyptian cat crouches with a dead mouse dangling by the tail from its paw. The whiskered face of the cat bears an expression of contentment that seems to mirror that of the monk.

Upright: A young man who is calm on the outside but inwardly intense and seething with determination. He likes to keep his purposes to himself and tends to be crafty and subtle. He works for his own ends with ruthless single-minded determination. His complete devotion to his own goals can generate mistrust and dislike in others.

Inverted: A young man who puts his pursuit of secrets and personal power above the welfare of others. This can lead him to unscrupulous conduct. He views others either as obstructions or tools to be used, and he displaces or uses them with utter ruthlessness. He hides his purposes to deceive. He does not think of himself as evil, but sees himself as clever and practical. He has scant sympathy for other human beings.

Knave of Cups: Scribe

A SLENDER EGYPTIAN nun who is scarcely older than a girl sits on a high stool before an angled wooden writing desk. She wears a white nemyss over her head, and a white linen robe, the loose sleeves of which have been tied up with black cords to prevent ink stains from ruining the garment. His cheeks are so hollow and his face so pale, she has a skulllike appearance. Around her neck on a chain hangs a pendant in the shape of an inverted triangle made of emerald. On a ledge of the writing desk rests a simple brass cup without a handle, from which extend several different reed pens, their shaped nibs stained with ink. Beside them is a small inkwell.

The scribe concentrates by the light of a brass oil lamp on a papyrus scroll spread across the desk. Beneath some writing at the top of the scroll may be seen an illumination in the shape of a mandorla. The papyrus beneath the mandorla is as yet still blank. Black ink smudges the sunken cheek and skinny fingers of the nun. Her fingernails are shaped into points, like the claws of a cat. The wall of the scriptorium in which she sits is covered with a crosshatch of pigeon holes, from many of which project rolled papyrus scrolls. The other holes are empty.

Upright: A young woman or child of a sweet, gentle disposition, tender of heart, kind and gracious toward others, with an unusually active imagination. Outwardly dreamy and sedate, her courage is aroused in fierce defense of those she loves. She is charming and loyal in friendship, faithful in love, a reliable companion.

Inverted: A young woman or child who tends to be indolent, disinclined to exert herself, loving luxury, self-absorbed, lost in her own fantasy and indifferent to the affairs of the real world. She puts her own ease and pleasure before the welfare of others. She is incapable of making herself useful and cannot be relied on. She is not so much selfish as caught up in herself and unable to see beyond her own desires and impulses.

rcenary — Thief

ades of yellow

King of Swords: Assassin

A SLENDER BUT athletic man has climbed partly through the tall open window of a house. He is dressed all in black, with a short silk tunic on his torso that has long sleeves down to his wrists, black leather gloves, and tight black trousers that fit into the tops of high black leather boots. At his waist a short, straight sword with a heavy silver pommel in the shape of a skull is belted in its scabbard. His silhouette, illuminated from the lamplight within the chamber, appears predatory. A skull mask covers the upper part of his face but leaves his mouth exposed. Slung across his back, he carries a short bow. From a chain around his neck hangs a pendant having the shape of an upright triangle made from ruby.

He leans forward into the room, mouth compressed into a grim line of concentration, and prepares to throw a dagger, holding the tip of the long, slender blade between the fingers of his right hand as he raises it beside his head for the cast. The blade of the knife has a dull finish to prevent it being easily seen against the darkness. His unsuspecting target is not visible but will soon be dead.

Upright: A mature man possessing cleverness and skill, with an active mind that seizes upon inspirations and immediately tries to realize them. He is fierce in pursuit of his purpose but may be frustrated due to his lack of foresight. He seldom thinks matters through, but rushes to attain his intention. His feelings are sensitive, but he tends to domineer over others merely by his force of will.

Inverted: A mature man who rushes in all directions at once and expends his force without useful result, distracted by petty details. Crafty and sly, he will use deceit to forward his goals and, if permitted to get away with it, will bully others into agreeing with him. When challenged, his boldness falls into confusion, and he is easily overcome by a firm determination.

Queen of Swords: Harlot

AN EGYPTIAN STREET prostitute stands in the open space in front of an ancient temple of the god Hermes. The temple has long been abandoned, and grasses grow up between the stone paving before the broken doors of the temple. A stone block that has tumbled from the roof may be seen behind her. She lounges beside a herm—a square column topped with the bearded head of Hermes, which is much weathered by age. The face of the god has a satyrlike expression. A white dove perches on top of the column. With one hand she raises the hem of her long green dress to reveal its red inner lining, along with her bare leg and thigh, while with her other hand she beckons. Her arms and legs are elaborately decorated with henna to inflame desire.

Her expression is hard and bold; her dark kohl-lined eyes seem to pierce like a blade and demand attention. Her rouged lips make some mocking remark. Long black hair hangs tangled and oily down her back and over her shoulder. Rings adorn the toes of her bare feet. From a chain around her neck hangs a pendant in the shape of an inverted triangle of sapphire. In the belt that surrounds her waist is thrust a long dagger, the pommel of which is silver, cast in the shape of a skull. Unnoticed by her, a little mongrel dog sniffs at her feet.

Upright: A mature woman who likes to dance and is fond of physical activities that require balance and grace. Her powers of perception are keen, and little escapes her notice. She makes an accurate interpretation of the situation and then acts decisively. Confident, precise, correct in her actions, but sometimes preoccupied with trifles.

Inverted: A mature woman outwardly attractive and graceful, but sly and unreliable, apt to make cutting and hurtful comments when she feels in a spiteful mood. She uses her personal appeal to manipulate others. Those who give their love or their loyalty to her often regret it. She never lets her affections get in the way of her advantage.

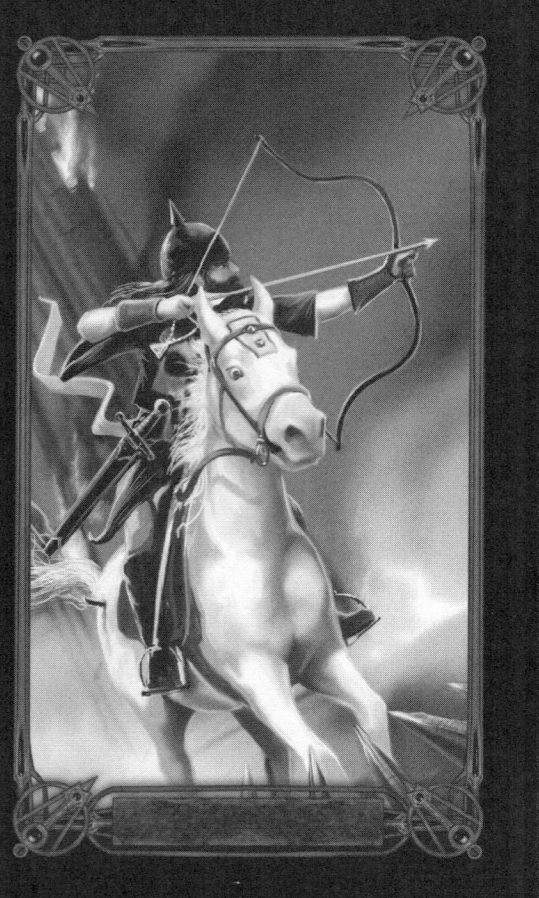

Knight of Swords: Mercenary

A MERCENARY SOLDIER with a black beard, who wears a spiked steel helmet and a battered steel breastplate over a worn leather tunic, guides a charging war horse with only his knees while drawing and preparing to fire a slender recurve war bow at the unseen enemy he attacks. He has minimal armor that is utilitarian rather than for show. The breastplate bears the raised image of a skull at its center. A pendant in the shape of an upright triangle of yellow topaz hangs from a chain around his neck. At his broad belt is a short, straight sword in a worn scabbard. A yellow silk scarf trails out behind him on the wind.

His scarred face glows with the exultation of battle as he prepares to release his arrow. The terrified steed rolls its eyes in frenzy as he urges it forward in a wild leap over the sharpened stakes of a picket fortification. The flank of the horse drips with blood from an arrow that has broken off in its wound. The air of the battlefield hangs heavy with smoke. In the background is visible a stone fortification tower, flames pouring up from its windows.

Upright: A young man with a sharp wit, clever, full of thoughts and ideas, restless in his interests, always seeking some new problem to occupy his attention. His eloquence may earn him the reputation of an expert. Idealistic, abstract in his thinking, sometimes absent-minded, he is more interested in the planning than the doing. He meticulously devises ways to reach his objective, but when he has it in his grasp, he loses interest.

Inverted: A young man who is fond of arguing for or against a thing merely for the pleasure of hearing himself talk but who holds no strong principles of his own. He likes to fence with words and delights in the clash of ideas. The truth does not matter to him very much—indeed, he has a difficult time recognizing it because he is able to rationalize both sides of any issue. He obstinately refuses to accept what does not suit his own purposes, and those who oppose him soon see the malicious side of his nature. He is apt to insult and browbeat those he cannot convince.

Knave of Swords: Thief

A YOUNG, SKINNY street urchin, with ragged and matted hair falling over her forehead, slyly looks to the side from the slits of charcoal-colored eyes as she cuts open the ties of a leather travel pack slung over the back of a donkey, and with her other hand extracts from it a chain with an emerald pendant in the shape of an inverted triangle. Her knife has a curved blade and a bone hilt that is carved on its end in the shape of a skull. She wears only a soiled dun cotton shirt pulled over her head, which hangs in tatters at its long tail around her naked thighs. An open sore runs with pus on her naked calf. Her face is feral in its fierceness.

The donkey watches the thief with one of its docile brown eyes. In front of the donkey is a table with a basket containing ripe pears, but the bridle of the donkey is tied to a post and is not long enough to allow the beast to eat from the basket.

Upright: A young woman or a child with an aggressive, combative personality. Practical of mind, she has great physical dexterity and control over her body. Others rely on her to settle disputes or to repair the effects of disasters. Her inner strength and determination inspire confidence. She can be remorseless in the pursuit of her purposes.

Inverted: A young woman or a child with a shallow, careless outlook on life and a tendency to use others to her advantage by means of cunning and trickery. Her pettiness defeats her even when she succeeds in her designs, since her victory accomplishes nothing of real worth. She is incapable of perceiving a larger purpose, but lives from day to day, exulting in her small triumphs. Beneath the surface she is troubled and unfulfilled.

Disks

Necromancer — Sorceress — Shaman — Auspex

Predominant color: shades of green

King of Disks: Necromancer

A MATURE BEARDED man stands within a magic circle marked in chalk on the floor of a crypt, cradling an open black book in his left arm. His long, graying hair falls over his shoulders. He wears a dark robe belted at the waist with a sash. On a chain about his neck hangs a pendant in the shape of an upright triangle of ruby. The only light comes from wax tapers set in holders on the floor around the circle. In his right hand he extends a golden pentacle toward a triangle marked in chalk on the flagstones a few feet away from the circle, holding the pentacle between all five fingers so that it is upright in his hand. The pentacle glows greenly with its own inner fire. On it is the Elder Seal. His lips part as he intones a chant of banishing. A sword lies within the circle at his slippered feet, broken into fragments.

Within the triangle, which points away from the circle, a demonic creature of spirit struggles to maintain its insubstantial form, its body distorted by the words of the chant and the radiance pouring forth from the pentacle of the necromancer. It can scarcely be distinguished from a plume of smoke, so incoherent has its form become, but its malevolent countenance, bent and elongated within the misty column, glares defiance at the necromancer as the thing struggles to overcome his will.

Upright: A mature man of a determined and patient disposition, capable of great physical industry. Most of his attention and energy is devoted to material matters of a practical nature. Reliable, skillful in mechanical things, usually serious and seldom given to spontaneous frivolous outbursts, he is regarded as somewhat dull by his friends, who nonetheless are glad enough to take advantage of his practical skills when they need them.

Inverted: A mature man with a grasping, avaricious nature, who is jealous of the success and wealth of others. He resents anyone who had done better in affairs of business or in the workplace, and expresses his resentment in mean and vulgar ways. Dull-witted, small-minded, meddling, seldom capable of higher principles or spiritual aspirations. He will never achieve great things because he wastes all his force on minor details.

Queen of Disks: Sorceress

A SLENDER WOMAN in a green dress embroidered with gold threads, her long black hair falling over her shoulders, stares down intently into the bowl of a large stone mortar as she grinds dry ingredients in it with a phallic-shaped stone pestle, using both hands. Arrayed on the wooden table around the pestle are a dead Egyptian scarab beetle, a dried asp, a mummified hand, and three large eggs, which stand upright on the table with no obvious means of support. The smallest egg, about the size of a hen's egg, is matte white. The egg of middle size is iridescent silver. The large egg, almost the size of an ostrich egg, is a glossy black speckled with flecks that resemble stars. Lying flat on the table is a circular cast-iron pentacle bearing within its circumference a version of the Elder Seal.

On the table before her, an open spell book bound in black leather gives her instruction in her work. It is illuminated by a candle burning in an iron candlestick. The tallow dripping down the sides of the candle has a curiously unhealthy color, a kind of greenish-yellow, suggesting an unnatural source. In the background of her workshop, bottles, jars, boxes, scrolls, a human skull, and other strange relics are to be dimly seen among the shadows. An owl perches on a wooden support in the shape of the letter T, watching the sorceress, who wears around her neck on a chain a pendant in the shape of an inverted triangle made of sapphire. She mutters an incantation as she grinds her powder, a look of intense concentration on her pallid face. Lurid greenish light shines up from the mortar as though the powder has self-ignited, and it limns her features from beneath.

Upright: A mature woman of a shy but charming and generous nature, always willing to extend her heart to others. Impetuous but timid, her sensible yet reserved manner causes her to be taken for granted by those who do not take the trouble to notice her true worth, which is considerable. She is intuitive rather than intellectual, but her intuition seldom fails her.

Inverted: A mature woman who devotes too much of her time and energy to unimportant repetitive labor. She grumbles about her lot in life but lacks the motivation to improve herself. Dull, unimaginative, with a pedestrian outlook on the world. She cannot conceive herself doing great things so she does not even try, but toils away slavishly under the instructions of others.

Knight of Disks: Shaman

TALL AND THIN, a black African shaman from the land of the Nile above the Egyptian Cataracts dances ritually on the beaten earth of the clearing in front of his mud-walled hut, shaking the tuft of black feathers tied to the tip of his thighbone wand at some unseen presence beyond the campfire that sends its red glow flashing over his sweat-covered bare limbs. His arms and legs are unnaturally thin, his face long and cheeks hollow. The hair of his head is shaved in a band from front to back, leaving only tufts of hair above each ear. His single garment is a loincloth made from woven grasses, but bands of feathers are bound around his ankles and upper arms.

The tiny white teeth in his small mouth, like the mouth of a child with unnaturally thin lips, and his sunken, glaring eyes cause his face to resemble an elongated skull. Around his neck hangs a bone whistle on a leather thong, and from a longer chain, a pendant in the shape of an upright triangle of yellow topaz. As he screams and gesticulates, he seems to be in the grip of some strange fit of possession. Fastened above the door of his hut behind him is a round wooden plaque bearing the carved image of the Elder Seal.

Upright: A young man with a prudent and practical attitude, who stays the course until its conclusion. He is best at handling material matters. He has little sense of humor and sometimes wonders what others find so amusing. He makes an excellent manager because of his talent for conserving resources and using them efficiently.

Inverted: A young man of limited imagination, who resents what he considers the affectations of intellectual and artistic types. He is slow to anger, but once his fury is aroused it cannot be controlled and often expresses itself through violence. He is concerned mostly about his health, appetites, and bodily needs. Once these are met, he lapses into a dull state of contentment, provided that nothing occurs that causes him to consider his own shortcomings.

Knave of Disks: Auspex

A YOUNG WOMAN stands behind a stone altar in the ruins of a pagan Egyptian temple, sunlight slanting down from great gaps in the fallen roof. She wears a ceremonial headdress with a solar disk in gold, upon which is engraved the Elder Seal. Her white linen robe is splashed on the front with fresh blood, from where it has spurted up from the sacrifice on the altar, which appears to be a white sheep or goat. Around the diviner's neck hangs a chain bearing a pendant in the shape of an inverted triangle of emerald. She holds the bloodstained sacrificial knife that has been used to slay and cut open the animal in her right hand.

The auspex elevates in her left hand the still-steaming liver of the sacrifice, having just used the knife to cut it free from the glistening viscera and entrails, which begin to drip blood over the sides of the altar.

She keenly regards the entrails in the bright sunlight, examining their shape and color. Her youthful face is struck with an expression of wonder, as if the most mysterious and precious secret in the world has just been revealed to her.

Upright: A young woman or a child of generous nature, caring of others, giving of herself, with a deep and constant courage to persevere in the face of difficulties. She preserves her resources with care, using them only where they are needed, and is able to act effectively when decisive action is required. She is seldom caught without ammunition.

Inverted: A young woman or a child who is vain of her looks and changeable in her affections. She squanders her resources with careless disregard for the future, merely for the pleasure of satisfying her vanity. Her own self-absorption makes her indifferent to the feelings of others. She assumes that everyone will be interested in her amusements and becomes petulant when they are called away on more important tasks.

Wands

Predominant color: shades of red

CHAPTER 6

✠

Number Cards

✠

Ace of Wands: Matrix of Fire

A SHORT, POWERFUL wand hangs vertically in the air, with a large crystal in the shape of a tetrahedron (three-sided pyramid) on its tip from which emanate seven colored rays that are the hues of the rainbow. Just below the base of the wand is the apex of a great Atlantean energy pyramid built from crystal blocks, in the sides of which these colors are reflected. The pyramid is the source of the wand's power.

Upright: Purpose, intention, motivation, determination, awakening will, beginning of an action, source, creation.

Inverted: False step, error, wrong-headedness, sterility, cut off at the root, stillbirth, squandered opportunity.

Two of Wands: Exaltation of Fire

AN ARISTOCRATIC ELDERLY man in rich robes stands lit by the ruddy rays of the morning sun between two ancient Atlantean pillars that form a kind of gateway, gazing across the surface of the ocean at a distant isle. The sunlight reflected on the water forms a shining path that links the isle with the pillared gate. On either side, heralds blow a summons on long, curved trumpets. Behind the elder, lost in thought, an attractive young noblewoman stands gazing downward into her hand at a richly jeweled pendant, the chain of which hangs around her neck.

Upright: Boldness, courage, resolution, determined will, personal authority, ambition, risk-taking.

Inverted: Pride, dominance, obstinacy, vengeful impulse, abuse of authority, dissatisfaction, impatience.

Three of Wands: Establishment of Fire

THE ATLANTEAN NOBLEWOMAN stands barefoot on the beach within a triangle formed by three staffs laid upon the sand, confronting a froglike male Deep One who remains in the water, which washes around his ankles. He had just emerged from the sea, and his naked body still glistens and drips. The two seem to have reached some sort of shared understanding.

Upright: Optimism, good prospects, auspicious progress, all according to plan, established enterprise, discovery.

Inverted: Suspension, disappointment, frustration, arrogance, excessive pride, self-assertion, unrealistic expectations.

Four of Wands: Manifestation of Fire

BENEATH A SCARLET canopy supported by four Atlantean pillars sit the noble lady and the Deep One side by side in a lovers' seat. He is clothed in royal robes of rich purple and gold. Their foreheads touch and they gaze amorously into one another's eyes, while before them, unnoticed, a young barbarian slave girl dances for their entertainment. Courtiers hover in the background, observing the tryst with nervous expectation.

Upright: Completion, perfection, settlement, celebration of success, conclusion of work, enjoyment, harmony, satisfaction.

Inverted: Unsteadiness, haste, insincerity, lack of preparation, anxiety about results, rushing to finish.

Five of Wands: Bitterness of Fire

TWO ATLANTEAN SOLDIERS wearing golden armor and richly colored tunics, who show the familiar first signs of the bloodline of crossbreeds between the Deep Ones and human beings, vanquish three barbarian warriors using short staffs surmounted with crystals that emit a powerful radiance. The barbarians quail and kneel in terror before the light, having cast down their three crude clubs and accepted their enslavement, at least for the present.

Upright: Contesting, strife, competition, struggle for dominance, testing by fire, grace under fire, honor toward foes.

Inverted: Harsh struggle, treachery, quarreling, cruelty, unfairness, taking advantage of others, manipulating the rules, cheating, legal maneuvers.

Six of Wands: Rule of Fire

AN ATLANTEAN MILITARY officer, completely human, dressed in splendid ceremonial armor and robes, walks with a crystal-tipped wand held upright in his right hand. In his left hand he holds the end of a tether attached to the neck of a naked barbarian, who is prodded to walk after the officer by a soldier with a similar wand, who shows the first signs of the bloodline of the Deep Ones in his face and body. In the background stand vigilant four soldiers in whose faces and postures the taint of the Deep Ones is much more evident, each holding before him a crystal-tipped power wand across his chest.

Upright: Victory, rewards of labor, pleasure after conflict, enjoying the spoils, triumphal celebration, success attained.

Inverted: Insolence, vainglorious display, betrayal, a traitor, an empty triumph, false honors, the wrong person elevated to power.

Seven of Wands: Ordeal of Fire

THE NOBLE ATLANTEAN officer stands on the defensive with a crystal-headed staff held before him, ready to fend off the attack of six common soldiers whose faces show the coarsening influence of the bloodline of the Deep Ones. The mixed bloods sneer derisively at the pureblooded human and threaten him with their power wands.

Upright: Courage in opposition, independent effort, possible victory, personal triumph, confronting a challenge, strong competition.

Inverted: Confusion, loss of direction, quarrels, obstacles, lack of leadership, anxiety, indecision, embarrassment, putting on a brave face.

Eight of Wands: Energy of Fire

EIGHT WANDS EXTEND in from the sides of the card, four on each side. From their crystals emanate destructive rays that cross in conflict. In the background is the ruined remnant of an energy pyramid.

Upright: Sudden force, swift action, movement, need for haste, important communication, revelation, cause for hope.

Inverted: Squalls, quarrels, hasty actions that are regretted, possible theft, intemperate words, clash of wills, insolence.

Nine of Wands: Stability of Fire

A SENIOR ATLANTEAN priest stands in an eight-sided pentacle formed by eight wands set upright on the ground with their crystals sending rays outward at an angle from their sides. In his left hand he holds an open book of golden leaves, from which he recites a potent war chant. In his right hand he raises a ninth wand that emits an enormous ray of power directly upward.

Upright: Unshakable strength, obstacles overcome, determination, resolve, steady force, recovery from sickness, iron will.

Inverted: Obstinacy, delay, doubt, lingering illness, continuing opposition, prolongation of difficulty, elusive victory, need for vigilance.

Ten of Wands: Burden of Fire

BENEATH THE SETTING sun a naked male Deep One walks into the waves of the sea, carrying over his shoulder a bundle of ten of the crystal-tipped power wands. His broad back is hunched, and his face is not visible. Behind him on the sand lies a dead Atlantean noble, his blood staining the sand and seeping into the waves so that they are reddened at their edges.

Upright: Overbearing force, oppression, burden of victory, duties, weight of responsibility, obligations, debt of honor.

Inverted: Many difficulties, false friends, selfishness, ill will, injustice, slander, possible failure of purpose, intrigues, loss of a lawsuit.

Cups

Predominant color: shades of blue

Ace of Cups: Matrix of Water

SILVER CHALICE VERTICAL in the air above a sea of blood. From its blood-filled bowl issues a fountain of blood in three streams. The two outer streams arch over and fall back into the sea, but the central stream extends upward and expands at its top into a large red rose.

Upright: Happiness, gentle pleasures, receptiveness, fertility, wellspring, fountain of youth, renewal, vitalization, purification.

Inverted: Instability, mutation, uncontrolled growth, excess, wildness, spoiling, surplus, waste.

Two of Cups: Devotion of Water

A DARK-HAIRED HIGH priestess of Bast pours red wine from her silver cup into the upheld cup of a youth in sandals and the richly colored tunic of a nobleman who kneels at her bare feet, a wreath of flowers around the long golden hair of his head, an expression of joy on his face. Between them in the background is a statue of the goddess Bast in the form of a cat, seated on a square pedestal.

Upright: Love, concord, affection, marriage, a happy home, union, harmony, soul mate, commitment.

Inverted: Folly, silliness, extravagance, inappropriate affection, puppy love, infatuation, hopeless devotion, love squandered, dissipation.

Three of Cups: Abundance of Water

THE YOUNG MAN, obviously drunk, dances between two laughing barelegged priestesses of Bast within a circle of flowers. One has her arm linked through his and is bare-breasted. The other, more discreetly clothed, is the high priestess who inducted him into the cult. She holds his opposite arm and pulls. They seem to be trying to tear him apart. Each of the three holds a brimming cup of red wine.

Upright: Abundance, good fortune, happy outcome, fulfillment, completion, enjoyment, celebration, rejoicing, merriment.

Inverted: Sensuality, excess, carried away, frenetic delight, Epicureanism, indulgence, excess, surfeit, reveling.

Four of Cups: Indulgence of Water

THE HEAD PRIESTESS holds out her wine cup, brimming with red wine, toward the young man, as though offering to fill his cup, but he turns his face away from her with an expression of dissatisfaction. His own cup droops in his hand near his groin, and the cup is obviously empty. In the background, a drunken man and a woman embrace lewdly and kiss near the statue of Bast, wine cups in their hands.

Upright: Restlessness, dissatisfaction, boredom, seeking after novelty, dalliances, weariness, loss of interest.

Inverted: Aversion, disgust, fatigue, emptiness, ennui, resentment, distaste, petulance, bitter dregs.

Five of Cups: Frustration of Water

THE HIGH PRIESTESS lies sprawled asleep across splendid silken pillows, her cup tipped over and spilling the dregs of its red wine at her side. On a low bed the other priestess and a youth lie together unconscious, their limbs entwined, four empty cups lying beside them. The young man stands some distance from the priestess with his back to her, his body modestly wrapped in a black cloak, his head bowed with dejection.

Upright: Disappointment, anxiety, sadness, hope dashed, bad news, unkind treatment, insult from a friend, troubled marriage, meager inheritance.

Inverted: Loss, deceit, treachery, ill will, broken friendship, failed project, inheritance withheld, pleasure denied.

Six of Cups: Satisfaction of Water

THE YOUNG MAN, barefoot and robed in the simple white linen of an acolyte, his head shaved, kneels within a temple of Bast to receive from the high priestess an empty silver chalice, which she presents to him on its side in both her hands. She wears a modest white linen robe trimmed in gold cloth, a serene expression on her face. Behind them is a darkened open archway leading into the inner sanctum of the temple of Bast. It is framed by two pillars, one of white alabaster stone and the other of red porphyry. Arrayed above the arch are five silver cups in the shape of a pentagram, their bowls pointing outward, stems toward the center.

Upright: Increase, gain, expectation of happiness, wish granted, renewed hope, awakened enthusiasm, new purpose, beginning of welcome changes.

Inverted: Smugness, unwarranted expectations, vanity, self-assertion, making demands, presumption, thanklessness.

Seven of Cups: Yearning of Water

THE YOUNG MAN has ventured through the arch into the inner sanctum of the temple, which suddenly has filled with radiance that obscures everything except a pentagonal array of five silver chalices in the air, encircling the head of what appears to the wondering acolyte to be the living goddess Bast, who stands beneath the pentagon of cups with the body of a beautiful woman but the head of a cat. Light emanates from the green eyes and tranquil countenance of the goddess. The young man extends his empty chalice in supplication, but the goddess makes a gesture of denial by holding her right palm flat above the open mouth of a chalice brimming with milk in her left hand.

Upright: Unfulfilled promises, visions of success, passive victory, error, deception, initial advantage is lost, empty sentiment, vain imaginings, wishful thinking.

Inverted: Drunkenness, selfish indulgence, lustfulness, deceit in love, dishonest friendship, hypocrisy.

Eight of Cups: Stagnation of Water

THE YOUNG ACOLYTE stands with his back to the goddess, silver chalice clutched close to his chest in both hands, a stubborn expression on his face. She extends her hand to him in welcome, but he does not see it. Arranged on the floor in a row on his right side are four silver chalices, tipped on their sides and empty, their bowls pointed away from him, and on his left side, three empty silver chalices in a row similarly tipped away from him.

Upright: Temporary success, one's own worst enemy, lack of motivation, a prize cast away, decline in interest, indolence.

Inverted: Success abandoned, self-defeat, immobility, paralysis, depression, misery.

Nine of Cups: Benediction of Water

THE CAT-HEADED GODDESS Bast, her breasts bared, pours streams of milk from two silver chalices that she holds on either side of her body at the level of her breasts. Each stream falls into three silver chalices arranged into a pyramid on the floor beneath, the milk in the upper chalice spilling over to fill the two lower chalices. The young acolyte kneels to the side of the goddess and holds out his chalice to intercept one of the streams, so that it overflows into the upper vessel of that pyramid and thence into the two chalices beneath.

Upright: Success realized, material pleasure, well-being, contentment, satisfaction, pride in achievement, wish achieved.

Inverted: Self-praise, full of oneself, vanity, self-congratulation, bragging, conceited, generous but foolish.

Ten of Cups: Fulfillment of Water

THE HIGH PRIESTESS and the acolyte stand facing each other on either side of a statue of Bast in the shape of a seated cat. He holds out in both his hands a silver chalice filled with white milk, preparing to sip from its brim, and she holds out a similar chalice filled with red wine. They gaze into each other's eyes across the chalices with understanding and affection, separated by the benevolent form of the goddess. He is enclosed in a crescent of four chalices filled with white milk that stand upon the floor at his feet, and she by an opposite crescent of four similarly arrayed chalices filled with red wine.

Upright: Success perfected, achievement realized, sustained happiness, wish completely fulfilled, heart's ease, ideal love, perfect friendship, cup runneth over.

Inverted: Wantonness, excess, drowning in pleasure, intemperance, lack of modesty, wastefulness, ingratitude, resentment.

Swords

Predominant color: shades of yellow

Ace of Swords: Matrix of Air

AN ELABORATE CEREMONIAL dagger with a broad, straight blade and a dragon-scale hilt floats vertically in the air with its point upward, the blade surrounded by a flickering aura that has the color of blood. Its pommel of yellowed human bone is carved in the shape of an inverted skull. Inhuman eyes glare above the metal crescent that forms its stylized guard. In the darkness behind it is the vague sense of a shadowy countenance, but only the red serpentine eyes have fully materialized.

Upright: Triumph, conquest, power for good, benign control, invoked force, intellectual clarity, penetration, force for good.

Inverted: Despotism, wrath, concentrated force, violation, overkill, domination, force for evil.

Two of Swords: Reconciliation of Air

BENEATH THE PALM trees in a garden at Damascus, a young Arabian nobleman with a handsome bearded face embraces a beautiful harlot with dark hair in a red dress. They have evidently just ceased to fight. His short, straight sword has slipped unnoticed from his hand to the pathway by his feet, and she holds a dagger drooping and forgotten at her side as they kiss with smoldering passion.

Upright: Truce, restoration of peace, differences resolved, quarrel ended, unselfishness, sympathy, understanding, balance achieved.

Inverted: Continuing tension, lingering resentment, tactlessness, disloyalty, imposture, unintended injury.

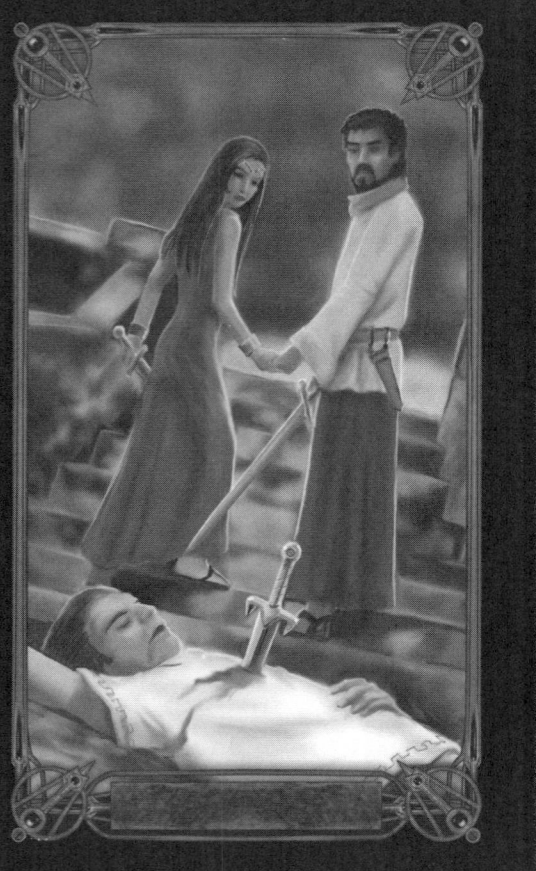

Three of Swords: Regret of Air

THE LOVERS CLASP hands and stand side by side, staring down at the corpse of the bearded man's rival for the harlot's affections. He grasps his drooping sword in his free hand, she her dagger. At his belt is an empty dagger sheath. Their mood is solemn as they contemplate the consequences of what they have done. Another dagger stands upright from the bloodied chest of the corpse, a foreign mercenary who was evidently surprised and killed before he could find a weapon with which to defend himself.

Upright: Absence, delay, disruption, sorrow, separation, tears, faithfulness, promise kept, honesty.

Inverted: Strife, mischief-making, evil pleasures, sowing discord, alienation, confusion, error.

Four of Swords: Repose of Air

THROUGH A DESERTED Damascus street, four mercenary soldiers carry a plain wooden coffin containing the corpse of their murdered comrade. Each holds his naked sword upright in his free hand. Their expressions are grim, their eyes vigilant as they search the shadowed doorways for potential threats.

Upright: Rest after struggle, end of worry, repose, convalescence, recovery, peacefulness, hermit's retreat, solitude, refuge.

Inverted: Need for vigilance, exile, appeasement, Danegeld, circumspection, precautions, safe house.

Five of Swords: Weakness of Air

THE BEARDED NOBLE lover crouches in the street, his arms raised in supplication, an expression of fear on his handsome face. His sword lies beside him in the dust. The four foreign mercenaries who carried the coffin of the dead lover to his grave stand around the man in threatening poses, swords directed at him, mocking his weakness with expressions of derision and contempt. His powerful family protects him from death, but not from humiliation.

Upright: Loss of dispute, defeat, failure, unfavorable ruling, display of weakness, troubles, anxiety for the future.

Inverted: Malice, spite, lies, mockery, poverty, avarice, cowardice, cruelty, dishonor, taking advantage of the weak.

Six of Swords: Scheming of Air

THE NOBLEMAN, HIS face bruised and cut from his latest encounter with the mercenary soldiers, pours gold pieces from a leather purse into the outstretched palm of an assassin who is dressed all in black. The assassin holds the end of his black silk scarf across his mouth and nose with his other hand to conceal his identity from his employer, and stares at the gold with hawklike eyes. A row of four narrow throwing knives is visible in a harness strapped around his upper arm. A long, straight sword is slung in its scabbard across his back, and a curved dagger hangs in its sheath from his belt.

Upright: Resolution, solution, labor, commission, task, confession, declaration, agent, envoy, hired hand, patience.

Inverted: Selfishness, conceit, expedient action, impatience, problem made worse.

Seven of Swords: Instability of Air

THE BOLD-HEARTED HARLOT steals a sword from its place on a rack that holds six swords, a grim expression on her face as she silently slips away with the naked weapon. It is her intention to avenge the humiliation of her lover. A sword-maker sits in the back of the shop at his grinding wheel, putting an edge on one of his weapons. He does not notice the presence of the woman in red.

Upright: Weak plan, unstable effort, half-hearted attempt, futility, vacillation, doubt, compromise, unreliable.

Inverted: Quarreling, obstruction, vain attempt, insolences, affronts, betrayal, untrustworthy, poor advice.

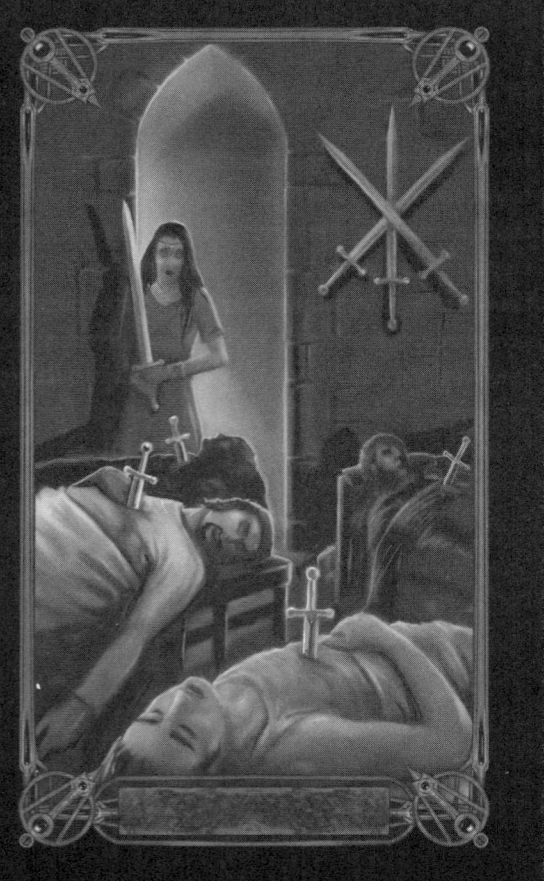

Eight of Swords: Constraint of Air

THE HARLOT STANDS in the doorway of a military barracks and stares with incomprehension at a scene of murder in the room beyond, her stolen sword forgotten in her hands. On the sleeping cots of the shadowed barracks, four mercenaries lie dead. A small throwing dagger projects from the heart of each corpse. On the wall hang three crossed swords.

Upright: Bad news, crisis, restriction, constraint, chagrin, the unforeseen, setback, small-mindedness.

Inverted: Fatal error, a prison, temporary bondage, pettiness, obsessed with details, interference, ill fortune.

Nine of Swords: Despair of Air

THE HARLOT AND the noble stand back to back. Her head is bowed in sorrow as she presses her palm to her brow. He wears an expression of discontent and irritation. It is evident that they have just argued. On the wall behind them is a yellow tapestry bearing an embroidered design that shows a row of nine swords, five pointing left and four pointing right. The swords slant toward the backs of the two figures.

Upright: Delay, deception, disappointment, shame, suspicion, suffering, loss, hardship, heartlessness, cruelty.

Inverted: Obedience, faithfulness, patience, endurance, resignation, acceptance, martyr-dom, persistence in the face of difficulty.

Ten of Swords: Abandonment of Air

THE BEARDED NOBLEMAN bends his neck as he kneels across a block beneath the enormous black sword of an official executioner, who wears a leather hood to conceal his face. The wrists of the young man are bound together. His face wears an expression of mingled terror and despair. Behind the raised wooden platform upon which the public execution is being enacted, nine arms brandish naked swords in the air.

Upright: Disruption, failure, defeat, ruin, affliction, loss of discipline, mental collapse.

Inverted: Insolence, impermanence, temporary authority, momentary advantage, time running out, unrealistic view, loss of touch with reality.

green

Ace of Disks: Matrix of Earth

AN INHUMAN HAND extends upward, its long fingers and blackened talons curling around a leaden disk that bears cast into its surface a detailed version of the Elder Seal.

Upright: Material gain, productive labor, wealth, prosperity, valued possessions, property.

Inverted: Burden of ownership, responsibilities, duties, danger of theft, anxiety about money, lack of trust.

Two of Disks: Inversion of Earth

A BEARDED NECROMANCER stands beside an open grave beneath the light of the waning crescent moon and watches while a naked black-skinned ghoul drags out the corpse of a woman, still wrapped in her linen shroud. Her face is covered but her sex is obvious by her slender waist and the fullness of her hips beneath the linen. The ghoul's clawed hands are well adapted to digging in the soil, and his thin limbs are much stronger than they appear, allowing him to easily wrest the corpse from its bed of earth. On two of the low stone tombstones of the cemetery is carved a simple version of the Elder Seal.

Upright: Change, transformation, alternation, cycles, gain and loss, harmonious revolution, ebb and flow, cheerfulness, recreation, rhythm of life, a message, a visit.

Inverted: Forced cheerfulness, unwelcome change, arguments, inconsistencies, downturn of fortunes, bad news, making the best of it.

Three of Disks: Purpose of Earth

AN ATTRACTIVE YOUNG sorceress creeps in stealth away from the corpse of an executed murderer, whose body has been hung within a tall and narrow iron cage on a gibbet at a crossroad as a warning to others. The left arm of the decaying corpse is missing its hand and forearm. She cradles this gruesome prize to her bosom as though it were an infant. From the base of the iron cage dangle three iron disks engraved with the shape of the Elder Seal.

Upright: Work, skilled labor, craft, constructive force, building up, erection, increase in material things, clever use of skills.

Inverted: Mediocrity, shoddy construction, incompetence, negligence, weakness, flawed work, hidden errors, impending malfunction.

Four of Disks: Generation of Earth

THE SORCERESS FASHIONS a hand of glory in her workshop. It stands upright on her table, the wasted hand of an executed murderer, its bony fingers extended upward like the naked limbs of some lightning-blasted tree. On the tip of each finger is a taper made from human fat, its tallow dripping down around the finger. She uses a wisp of straw to light the candles from the flame of an oil lamp that illuminates her worktable. On the table surface lie four silver medallions inscribed with the Elder Seal.

Upright: Dominion, rank, earthly power, legacy, inheritance, property, guarding possessions, a safe, vault, strongbox, gain of money.

Inverted: Covetous, stingy, suspicious, unoriginal, unenterprising, miserly, narrow-minded, pennywise and pound-foolish, no prospects for advancement.

Five of Disks: Trouble of Earth

THE NECROMANCER HUNCHES his shoulder and pulls his cloak around him as he walks along a street away from three ragged and dirty-faced peasant children of various ages, who throw stones at his back and mock and jeer at him. The man's bearded face is dark with anger and the promise of future malice. In his arm he cradles protectively a large black book, the cover of which bears five disks, each inscribed with the Elder Seal.

Upright: Loss of a job, material troubles, bad investment, business worries, moral support, understanding, friend in need, shared difficulties, determination.

Inverted: Destitution, bankruptcy, loss of possessions, ruin, chaos, discord, friendlessness, obstinacy, blaming others.

Six of Disks: Reception of Earth

THE SORCERESS PASSES the completed hand of glory to the necromancer, who stands on the side of a deserted road under a dead tree. He receives it while at the same time extending her payment with his other hand. Upon his palm rests a fresh human heart somewhat below the adult size, suggesting that it is the heart of a child. Each stares meaningfully into the eyes of the other but no words are spoken. Six disks carved with the Elder Seal hang from the limbs of the dead tree.

Upright: Power, influence, rank, title, achievement, success, prosperity, time in the sun, material gains, ventures prosper, generous and just.

Inverted: Insolence, patronage, buying favors, bribes, misuse of funds, abuse of position, favoritism, cronyism, corruption.

Seven of Disks: Squandering of Earth

THE NECROMANCER STANDS in a posture of frustration within a large and elaborate chalk circle drawn on the stone floor of his vault, the fingers of his right hand like claws as he tries to command the soul of a young woman back into her corpse. The body lies at his feet, half within the circle, her shroud peeled back to reveal her death-pale face and naked shoulders. The spirit of the woman, a glowing cloud of light, flees away from the necromancer with an expression of horror upon its partially formed features. He brandishes the hand of glory like a macabre yet impotent weapon. Seven disks bearing the simplified Elder Seal are arrayed around the circle.

Upright: Blighted hopes, good money after bad, unfulfilled expectations, disappointment, scant gains, unprofitable labor.

Inverted: Misery, enslavement, necessity, loss of place, humble condition, betrayal of trust, business dispute, failed enterprise.

Eight of Disks: Analysis of Earth

THE WOMAN'S CORPSE lies on a table in the necromancer's vault. He has laid her torso open and studies with intent gaze her organs and entrails strewn out over her corpse, which glow with a strange light of their own. The hand of glory burns on a stand behind him. On his arm he cradles the great black book, open for reference to a page bearing the Elder Seal. Seven similar seals are carved along the edge of the table.

Upright: Skill, craftsmanship, care over details, employment, a commission, industriousness, agriculture, excessive prudence, management of assets.

Inverted: Avariciousness, hoarding, meanness, fear of risk-taking, lacking in enterprise, too much attention to small things, low cunning.

Nine of Disks: Fulfillment of Earth

THE SHADE OF the dead woman, naked and glowing with a soft cool light beneath the waning rays of the horned moon, stands beside the necromancer and gestures to a spot under a square stone obelisk where a black-skinned ghoul has dug the ground, unearthing a buried strongbox. Her posture is subdued and sad. The face of the necromancer glows with exultation. He starts eagerly toward the box while the ghoul holds up a large golden medallion on a chain it has just drawn from the interior. The medallion bears the Elder Seal. Eight similar seals appear on the breast of the necromancer's ceremonial robe.

Upright: Inheritance enjoyed, increase in possessions, material gain, wise management, security.

Inverted: Ill-gotten gains, crassness, covetousness, vulgarity of display, mismanagement, enterprise in difficulty, theft.

Ten of Disks: Possession of Earth

THE NECROMANCER STANDS beneath the stars with face and arms upraised in mighty invocation. Around his neck hangs the medallion with the Elder Seal. In the night sky above his head, an enormous dark face stares down at him, its features vague and distorted as though it were just manifesting. The body of the necromancer is surrounded by the glowing bodies of familiar spirits who fly around his torso and limbs, trailing their ethereal substance behind them like serpents. The great book rests opened on a reading stand before him. The back of the stand bears the Elder Seal. Behind him on each side are stone pillars that frame him as though in an open doorway. Each pillar bears four images of the Elder Seal.

Upright: Family affairs, the homestead, wealth, retirement, pension, a gift, end of work, prudent investment.

Inverted: Dullness of wit, lack of enterprise, sloth, loss, robbery, inability to handle money, end of gain, gambling debts.

THE NECRONOMICON TAROT can be used for any of the standard divination methods that you will find in other books on the tarot. The technique presented here is original and relies on the dynamic interaction between the trumps and the suit cards. As a general rule in divination, the trumps represent higher forces and cosmic principles, whereas the suit cards stand for human beings and the events in their lives. This is only a rule of thumb for using the cards in practical divination, since each card has both a higher and a lower aspect to its nature, but it does not hurt to think of the trumps as cosmic in their significance, and the suit cards as earthly.

The Necronomicon Layout is designed to provide a general life reading into the present and immediate future situation of the inquirer. It gives insight into five areas: Family Life, Social Life, Work Life, Love Life, and School Life.

CHAPTER 7

✢

Divination

✢

Divide the deck into two packs, one containing the twenty-two trumps and the other containing the fifty-six suit cards. Shuffle both packs thoroughly, taking care to break them into two parts every now and then and rotate one of the packets, so that there is a good mix of upright and inverted cards. This layout takes into account the meanings of inverted cards. However, those who prefer not to employ inverted cards (which are known as reversals) in divination can simply keep all the cards upright when shuffling the two packs, and read them all upright in the layout. It is a matter of personal preference.

Taking reversals into account will generally make a reading less positive, and if too much emphasis is placed on the significance of inverted cards, the reading can become so bleak and depressing that it loses all usefulness. The diviner should be aware of this danger and avoid overly stressing the hurtful aspect of inverted cards. This is especially true when using the *Necronomicon Tarot* for divination, because many of the images are darker and more threatening than those of a regular tarot.

Reversal has the effect of weakening the purity or forcefulness of a card. As a result, a generally favorable card becomes less favorable when it is reversed. However, when a generally harmful card is reversed, the same weakening action can make it slightly less bad. Sometimes the action of reversal causes the pure meaning of a card to be corrupted or partially obscured, like a lamp viewed through a dirty pane of glass. As a result, a reversed card may take on a slightly different, but still related, meaning to its significance when upright. Reading reversals is a bit of an art, which is perhaps why some diviners prefer to avoid them entirely.

Take up the pack of suit cards and deal out a row of five cards facedown from left to right. Set the pack aside. Take up the pack of trumps and deal a similar row of five cards facedown above the first row, also from left to right. Lay a sixth card from the trumps facedown above the middle card in the upper row, and set the pack aside. The upper row is known as the Masters. The lower row is known as the Servants. The single card at the top is called the Card of Fate.

The first Master on the left is the trump of the Family Life of the inquirer, and the Servant immediately below it pertains to relatives and family members. The second Master rules the Social Life of the inquirer, and its Servant deals with friends or acquaintances. The third Master concerns the Work Life, and its Servant gives insight into coworkers, bosses, and subordinates. The fourth Master is the card of the Love Life, and its Servant pertains to the love or spousal interest of the inquirer. The fifth Master is about the School Life, and its servant gives insight into teachers, guides, or mentors. The solitary Card of Fate that stand above all the others shows a ruling higher influence over the immediate future of the inquirer that may affect any of these five areas of life.

The upper row of Masters pertains to the present situation. It gives the environment or framework of the inquirer's life in which events unfold and actions are taken. The lower row of Servants shows the near future, things that will occur to cause changes to the existing circumstances, and the individuals most concerned with those events. The Card of Fate is timeless and may affect both present and future conditions.

When the number cards of the suits from Ace to Ten turn up on the row of Servants, they define the events in which the classes of people in that area of the inquirer's life will play a part. When a court card turns up on the row of Servants, it indicates an individual who will dominate that area of life in the near future. The presence of a court card shows that the person it represents will be more important in the

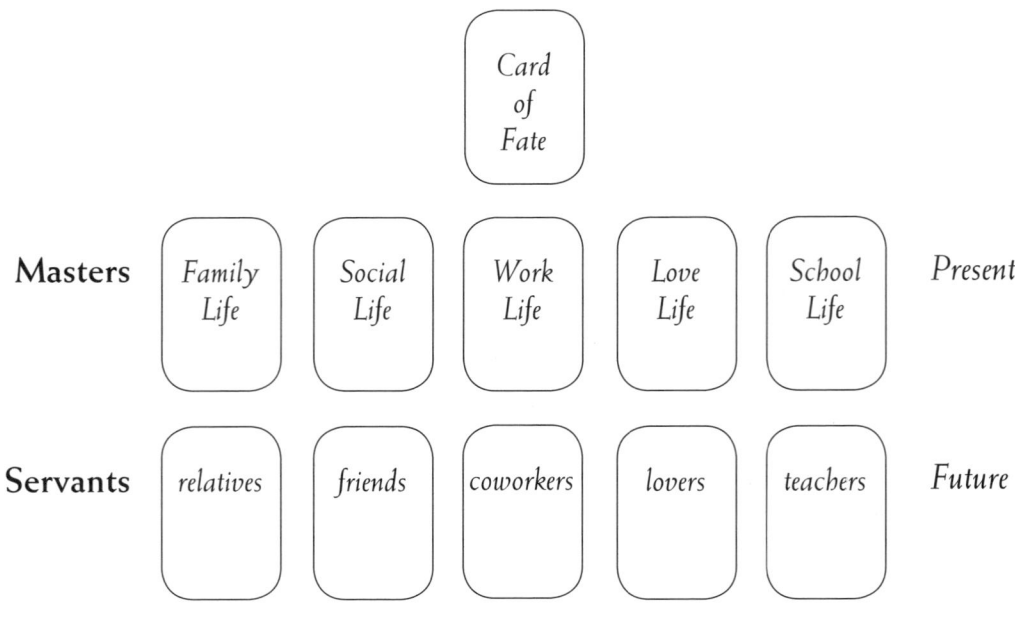

Necronomicon Layout

life of the inquirer than the events connected with the person.

For example, the Servant under the Master of Family Life shows the actions of relatives and family members in the home environment. If it is a number card, it indicates particular actions taken by a relative or family member; but if it is a court card, it identifies a specific individual who is a relative or family member, who will be more important in the life of the inquirer than the near-future events surrounding the person.

The Card of Fate is a kind of a wild card that can be used as the key to understanding the layout. It should be considered in conjunction with each pair of Master and Servant, as a link between them that influences and defines their dynamic interaction. The Master gives the background as it presently exists in that particular area of life. The Servant shows the future unfolding of events that grow out of the present situation, emphasizing either the events themselves in the case of a number card, or the person at the center of those events in the case of a court card. The Card of Fate suggests how the future may have evolved out of the present.

The Card of Fate also shows, in a more general sense, the overall direction of the inquirer's life in the near future, its prevailing tendency or inclination. It should be turned first and considered by itself at the beginning of a reading, to obtain the keynote for the interpretation of the layout, and also considered alone at the end of the reading, as the final summation of the message of the cards concerning the inquirer's life. It is not a card of fatality, but should be taken as a guide and a warning. If it is positive, the trend in the near future will be positive in general, but if it is negative, the trend will be more difficult and will require caution and thoughtfulness in the area indicated by the Card of Fate.

First, turn the Card of Fate upright from left to right to preserve its orientation. Consider its general significance in the life of the person receiving the reading. The remaining cards are read from left to right, in pairs. Turn each pair over from side to side to ensure that their orientation is maintained—that upright cards remain upright and reversed cards remain reversed. First turn the Master and consider its significance in the context of the area of life it rules, then turn the Servant below it and analyze its relationship to the Master. Think of how it evolved out of the Master and how the Master influences and constrains its action. Now consider the influence of the Card of Fate in conditioning the link between the Master and the Servant.

The Master of each pair is passive or background; the Servant is the active agent that functions within the frame of the Master. The Servants all represent people in the life of the inquirer, with emphasis either on what they will do in the case of the number cards, or who they are in the case of the court cards. The Card of Fate acts as a filter that limits and colors the dynamic between each Master and Servant. Depending on its nature, the action of each pair may be strong or weak, assisted or hindered, constructive or obstructive.

When all the cards are faceup on the table, look across the line of the Masters for any trend or common thread that connects all five cards. Then study the line of Servants for any common trend—for example, a predominance of a particular suit, or several court cards. Two court cards side by side may indicate two people working together, either in cooperation or in conflict, in the life of the inquirer. Aces generally signify an initiative or a new beginning, whereas Tens signify a completion or conclusion and the closure it brings. The Wands as a group are willful and enterprising, the Cups are emotional and affectionate, the Swords are intellectual and divisive, and the Pentacles are tangible and materialistic.

The Master of the Family Life shows the personal living environment of the inquirer. This will usually be a house or an apartment, but in general is wherever the person sleeps for the night. It also pertains to the family homestead, particularly in the case of those who have not yet fully moved away from that environment, such as a university student living in a dormitory at university. It is the place of the family where living is done. The Servant shows the actions of other family members as they bear on the future life of the inquirer. It encompasses immediate family members such as father, mother, brothers, and sisters, as well as relatives such as uncles, aunts, and cousins. In general it bears only on blood relations, the exception being close adopted family members.

The Master of the Social Life is the background environment in which the inquirer seeks social amusement when not at home or at work. It pertains to regular haunts such as clubs, the houses of friends, bars or taverns where a lot of time is spent, and any hangout where the inquirer goes to relax and have fun. Its Servant shows the actions of acquaintances and friends. It does not so much bear on very close friends, but has to do with more casual friendships of social convenience. These are the people the inquirer interacts with in various social settings, apart from his family and relatives.

The Master of Work Life reveals the nature of the work environment in which the inquirer pursues his career or earns his living. It may be an office, a factory floor, or a more flexible and variable environment in the case of those whose careers cause them to work outside, or to move from place to place, such as surveyors, road workers, or real-estate agents. The Servant expresses the future actions of coworkers, subordinates, and superiors in the workplace, those who interact with the inquirer at work.

The Master of the Love Life pertains to the environments in which the inquirer seeks loving companionship with an individual who is very close emotionally. This may be a bedroom, a car, a houseboat, a summer cabin, a lover's apartment: any environment where love is shared. The Servant shows the actions of a lover or spouse, or more rarely a very close friend with whom ties of love that may not be sexual are shared. The Master is where the heart is, and the Servant is the person to whom the heart is given.

The Master of the School Life reveals the nature of the intellectual environment, where the mind is exercised and developed. It may be a school or university, or it may be simply where study is done, such as a library or favorite reading place. It is the times and circumstances when intellectual activity takes place, when plans are made and goals in life are established. It may even be as unstructured as the circumstances under which the inquirer is compelled to reassess his

or her life. The Servant pertains to teachers, guides, and mentors, those who assist or direct the process of learning.

Although all five of the Masters have been described in terms of physical environments, they also reveal the inner environments of the inquirer in these five areas of life. The Master of the Family Life, for example, is the sense of family and home that the inquirer carries around in memory, and experiences in thought and emotion. The Master of the Love Life is the inquirer's inner state of love, affection, tenderness, sharing, that he or she enters from time to time, just as one might walk into a room. It would be just as well to refer to these five areas of life as zones of experience. The external environment of each only takes on its particular qualities when the internal state of thought and feeling is achieved that corresponds with it. A home is only a home because it feels homelike. A workplace is only a place of work because we go there prepared to work.

One advantage of the Necronomicon Layout compared with those usually given in books on the tarot is that it fully utilizes the trumps. When the entire deck of cards is shuffled together and laid out in a card spread, the trumps will usually be few in number and scattered throughout the spread. The Necronomicon Layout is designed to give the trumps the importance they deserve in divination, which is greater than their number suggests. There may be only twenty-two trumps and fifty-six suit cards, but the trumps are half the tarot in their significance, a fact often lost in tarot divination.

To Write to the Author or Artist

If you wish to contact the author or artist or would like more information about this book, please write to the author in care of Llewellyn Worldwide and we will forward your request. The author, artist, and publisher appreciate hearing from you and learning of your enjoyment of this book and how it has helped you. Llewellyn Worldwide cannot guarantee that every letter written to the author or artist can be answered, but all will be forwarded. Please write to:

Donald Tyson & Anne Stokes

℅ Llewellyn Worldwide
2143 Wooddale Drive,
Dept. 978-0-7387-1086-0
Woodbury, MN 55125-2989

Please enclose a self-addressed stamped envelope for reply, or $1.00 to cover costs. If outside U.S.A., enclose international postal reply coupon.

Many of Llewellyn's authors have websites with additional information and resources. For more information, please visit our website:

WWW.LLEWELLYN.COM

LLEWELLYN ORDERING INFORMATION

Order Online:
Visit our website at www.llewellyn.com, select your books, and order them on our secure server.

Order by Phone:
- Call toll-free within the U.S. at 1-877-NEW-WRLD (1-877-639-9753). Call toll-free within Canada at 1-866-NEW-WRLD (1-866-639-9753).
- We accept VISA, MasterCard, and American Express

Order by Mail:
Send the full price of your order (MN residents add 6.875% sales tax) in U.S. funds, plus postage & handling to:

**Llewellyn Worldwide
2143 Wooddale Drive
Woodbury, MN 55125-2989**

Postage & Handling:
Standard (U.S. & Canada). If your order is:
$24.99 and under, add $4.00
$25.00 and over, FREE STANDARD SHIPPING

AK, HI, PR: $16.00 for one book plus $2.00 for each additional book.

International Orders (airmail only):
$16.00 for one book plus $3.00 for each additional book

*Orders are processed within 2 business days.
Please allow for normal shipping time. Postage and handling rates subject to change.*

NECRONOMICON

Donald Tyson

THE FIRST NECRONOMICON created in the true spirit of H. P. Lovecraft!

Anyone familiar with H. P. Lovecraft's work knows of the *Necronomicon*, the black magic grimoire he invented as a literary prop in his classic horror stories. There have been several attempts at creating this text, yet none stand up to Lovecraft's own descriptions of the *Necronomicon*…until now.

Fans of Lovecraftian magic and occult fiction will delight in Donald Tyson's *Necronomicon*, based purely within Lovecraft's own fictional universe, the Cthulhu Mythos. This grimoire traces the wanderings of Abdul Alhazred, a necromancer of Yemen, on his search for arcane wisdom and magic. Alhazred's magical adventures lead him to the Arabian desert, the lost city of Irem, ruins of Babylon, lands of the Old Ones, and Damascus, where he encounters a variety of strange creatures and accrues necromantic secrets.

0-7387-0627-2
$17.95
7 x 10, 288 pp., illus.

ALHAZRED
AUTHOR OF THE NECRONOMICON

Donald Tyson

H. P. LOVECRAFT'S compelling character Abdul Al-hazred is brought to life in this epic tale detailing the mad sorcerer's tragic history and magical adventures. Alhazred tells his own life story, beginning with himself as a poor, handsome boy in Yemen who attracts the attention of the king for his divine skill in poetry. As the court poet, young Abdul lives a luxurious life at the palace, where he studies necromancy and magic. But falling in love with the king's daughter leads to a foolish tryst that is ultimately discovered. As punishment, Abdul is tortured, brutally mutilated, and cast into the desert, known as the Empty Space. Battling insanity, he joins a tribe of ghouls and learns forbidden secrets from a stranger called Nyarlathotep. Thus begins his downward spiral into wickedness. Renamed Alhazred, he escapes the desert and embarks on a quest to restore his body and reunite with his true love. Traveling across the ancient world and fantastic realms, he is hounded by foes and tormented by the demands of his dark lord.

0-7387-0892-5
$29.95
7 x 10, 696 pp.

Free Tarot Readings

✠

Visit our website at
http://www.llewellyn.com/free/
for free tarot readings!

Secrets
of the
NECRONOMICON